THE NEXT 7 GREAT EVENTS OF THE FUTURE

And What They Mean to You

D1473062

Randal Ross

THE NEXT 7

GREAT EVENTS OF THE FUTURE

AND WHAT THEY MEAN TO YOU

CREATION
HOUSE
Orlando, FL

THE NEXT 7 GREAT EVENTS OF THE FUTURE by Randal Ross
Published by Creation House
Strang Communications Company
600 Rinehart Road
Lake Mary, FL 32746
Web site: http://www.creationhouse.com

Unless otherwise noted, all Scripture quotations are from
the Holy Bible, New International Version. Copyright ©
1973, 1978, 1984, International Bible Society. Used by permission.

Scripture quotations marked KJV are from the King James
Version of the Bible.

Scripture quotations marked NKJV are from the New King
James Version of the Bible. Copyright © 1979, 1980, 1982 by
Thomas Nelson Inc., publishers. Used by permission.

Copyright © 1997 by Randal Ross
All rights reserved.
Printed in the United States of America
Library of Congress Catalog Card Number:97-65690
International Standard Book Number: 0-88419-457-4
78901234 BBG 876543

First printing, May 1997
Second printing, June 1997

To Delmar and Phyliss Ross . . .

To my mother who taught me how to love God
with my whole heart . . .
To my father who taught me how to be
the friend of God.

Acknowledgments

When God placed the subject matter of this book on my heart to write, He also graciously surrounded me with very capable men and women with servant's hearts to encourage and assist me. I wish to thank Don Ketcherside, my fellow staff member at Trinity Church, who so persistently worked on research. A very special thanks to Alyse Lounsberry of Creation House who, with diligence and godly insight, labored to edit the messages and material I brought to her.

To my family—my congregation—at Trinity Church in Lubbock, Texas, I gratefully acknowledge your support, enthusiasm, and encouragement to do my best to present God's message with clarity and boldness to this generation, so that we may be that Bride of Christ, washed in His precious blood, our hearts prepared and eagerly awaiting that first glimpse of His face.

Contents

THE NEXT 7 GREAT EVENTS OF THE FUTURE

Contents

Preface

I admit it—*I used to be a "prophecy freak."* You know all about "prophecy freaks"— they're the ones who eat, sleep, breathe, and dream about nothing but the End Times. They study, then quote all the End-Time Scripture passages. They talk about nothing but Bible prophecy. They are walking encyclopedias crammed full of the latest facts, figures, and formulas. They think about them continually. They attend every End-Time conference there is.

Don't get me wrong—there's nothing wrong with taking an interest in the study of the End Times. But taken to the extreme, too much concentration on

End-Time events can mean an absence of balance.

Ever been there? Ever met someone who *was?* That's where I was for awhile—out of balance, teetering on the edge of extremism, staring down at the deep end of the pool. Let me tell you what snapped me out of it.

In the seventies, a well-known prophecy teacher came to town. He had a bunch of charts that, by their very official-looking nature, made him appear as authoritative as a rocket scientist on the subject of the End Times. To me, this man appeared to have the study of the End Times down to a fine science. I listened attentively as this gentleman talked, tracked, and charted . . . . and pretty soon, he even came up with an official-sounding date for the Rapture—the day the Lord will come for His own, that glorious day when Christians will be taken out of the earth. As I listened to his teachings along these lines, I became disturbed in my spirit as the Holy Spirit reminded me that Jesus said no man would know for certain when that day would occur, but that when certain signs became evident in the earth, we would know the *season,* and that the day was *near* (Luke 21:8–11).

Yet this well-meaning teacher, so full of zeal, fixed July 28, 1978, as the official date for the Rapture.

The news raged through town like wildfire. Everyone was so excited—even me. After all, the months preceding the Great Day had been pretty amazing. The church where this man was holding his meetings had not just grown—it had exploded. People had just started flocking there from the highways and byways, and as the Great Day drew

Preface

near, every service was packed out. Those who heard this man's preaching were filled with hope and expectation. Things were going great. Or so it seemed. . . .

But something about all that zeal just didn't ring true in my spirit. I couldn't seem to buy in totally to what this man was claiming. I remember observing all these goings on and thinking, *I wish I knew for sure when He was coming.*

As we edged closer to July 28, 1978, people began doing some mighty strange things. Some sold their homes. Some quit their jobs. Some even divorced their spouses. Again, as I observed the strange stuff going on around me, I thought, *This is not right!*

Then came the Great Day. The church made a big deal out of what was sure to come, and held a Rapture-Day picnic on the main drag of town. Believers were elated. Moms and dads and kids and grandparents turned out for the event, dressed in their starched-and-pressed Sunday best, toting dishes of potato salad, fried chicken, and all the trimmings so they could enjoy some last-minute food and fellowship while waiting to go up.

Everyone, it seemed, was ready to go—all clean and neat and bright and smiling. But the happy atmosphere began to deteriorate as the day dragged on . . . and no Rapture. Little spats broke out between the expectant. There was even some fighting over the highest ground, and who got to stand there so they would be the *first* to go.

By the end of the day, the clothes were wrinkled, the food eaten, and the smiles faded. When nothing at all glorious had happened on that day, the downcast crowd filtered on home.

Church attendance dropped off dramatically in proportion to the horrible disappointment experienced by the Rapture Day adherents. Some of the believers bounced back; some did not. There was much confusion and heartache, and some of the wounded ones just quit coming to church. They fell away. The damage to the body of Christ was enormous. People became angry with God and the church. Marriages were torn apart, households up-ended, lives shipwrecked.

Seeing the end result of this prophecy madness, I became determined to reject all study of biblical prophecy. All prophecy seemed to do was *hinder* more than help, *discourage* more than encourage, *confuse* more than clarify. I had seen the dangerous extremes and had witnessed the damage firsthand. I was more than wary. So I put the study of prophecy and the End Times on the shelf, and I refused to take it down.

Many of us have friends who went off the deep end at some point over Bible prophecy. These individuals lost their perspective and were taken out of fellowship for a period of time for their unbalanced theological views. I didn't want that to happen to me or to my congregation.

So I held at arm's length the study of prophecy—that is, until one day the Lord told me: "You have to study prophecy because there is something beyond the spectacular that I am going to do in these last days." In obeying God, I allowed the Holy Spirit to teach me about prophecy, and He gave me fresh revelation regarding seven great events that are poised to occur in the time

Preface

remaining until Christ returns to rule and reign in righteousness. In the course of studying prophecy from this new perspective, I recaptured some of the old excitement as I realized that it is not prophecy but *imbalance* that produces the fruit of frustration, confusion, and division. These things are not what Jesus intended to accomplish with this vital gift to the body of Christ.

Jesus is not about sowing division through the gift of prophecy but about using that gift to bring healing, help, and clarity to His plan for earth during these critical End Times.

As we draw near to the year 2000 and the threshold of a new millennium, the importance of prophetic literacy and balance will only increase. The year 2000 will bring with it a revival of prophetic activity, and this revival will be accompanied by both enormous potential and grave danger. We must rightly divide the Word of truth. We must adequately discern what the Spirit of the Lord is saying to the church in what may amount to the final few minutes of earth-time remaining on God's eternal timeclock.

May this message about the next seven great events of the future be a blessing to you. May it help you to see more clearly what God is saying to the church in the final few minutes of earth-time remaining before His glorious return.

Randal Ross
Lubbock, Texas 1997

Introduction:

THE PROPHECY BOMB

And Jesus went out, and departed from the temple: and his disciples came to him for to show him the buildings of the temple. And Jesus said unto them, See ye not all these things? Verily I say unto you, There shall not be left here one stone upon another, that shall not be thrown down. And as he sat upon the mount of Olives, the disciples came unto him privately, saying, Tell us, when shall these things be? and what shall be the sign of thy coming, and of the end of the world?

And Jesus answered and said unto

*them, Take heed that no man deceive you.
For many shall come in my name, saying,
I am Christ; and shall deceive many.*

*And ye shall hear of wars and rumors
of wars: see that ye be not troubled: for all
these things must come to pass, but the
end is not yet. For nation shall rise against
nation, and kingdom against kingdom:
and there shall be famines, and pestilences, and earthquakes, in divers places.*

*All these are the beginning of sorrows.
Then shall they deliver you up to be
afflicted, and shall kill you: and ye shall
be hated of all nations for my name's
sake. And then shall many be offended,
and shall betray one another, and shall
hate one another. And many false prophets
shall rise, and shall deceive many.*

*And because iniquity shall abound, the
love of many shall wax cold. But he that
shall endure unto the end, the same shall
be saved. And this gospel of the kingdom
shall be preached in all the world for a
witness unto all nations; and then shall
the end come.*

—Matthew 24:1–14

Matthew, chapter 24—one of the most significant,
prophecy-loaded passages in the entire New
Testament—came forth as the result of an innocent question the disciples asked of their Master
during an afternoon stroll.

Here they are—Jesus and His disciples—gathered

in Jerusalem to attend the Passover festivities. Everybody's having a great time. Jerusalem is packed with pilgrims from throughout the land of Israel, all flocking into town for the holy holiday.

But Jesus has been under pressure. Attacks against Him are on the increase. The Pharisees manage to lay snares in His way almost daily, hoping to catch Him in the midst of some act that will most surely brand Him as what they have already determined Him to be—heretic . . . impostor . . . infidel . . . phony Messiah . . . fake. It is the final week of His life, and His heart grows heavy with the weight of what most certainly is to come. He knows that the agony of the cross looms just ahead. And here, while His focus is fixed firmly on eternal matters, His disciples want to party and talk politics.

He's focusing in on Calvary, trying to prepare Himself for inevitable death—His earthly destiny. And the disciples are admiring the temple and commenting on its beauty and symmetry. No doubt as they ramble on about this magnificent earthly temple, Jesus grows quiet for a moment as He turns inward at the disciples' lack of insight into that which is just ahead for their Lord and Master.

"Come on, Jesus, lighten up!" one of the disciples may have suggested.

"Look at this gorgeous temple! Aren't these stones something else?"

And that's when Jesus drops the prophecy bomb.

Boom! Matthew, chapter 24 just came spilling forth

from Jesus' lips, turning upside down forever any ideas the disciples may have still harbored of a political, earthly kingdom or an imminent earthly reign of Jesus—their Messiah. Annihilated was any regard for a physical temple where formal worship would take place.

Here was Jesus—out of the clear blue sky— exploding every myth the disciples may have still held regarding His physical reign as King of Kings and Lord of Lords. Here was Jesus, blowing up every one of their existing schemes for rebellion and insurrection against the Roman government.

On a pleasant afternoon, during a casual stroll around the perimeter of the temple mound, Jesus pointed to the stones of the temple Solomon built and said, "See these stones? Get a good look— because not one of these stones will be left standing after I complete what I came here to do!"

Boom! There goes long-held religious tradition! Boom! There goes all regard for those beautiful man-made stones! Jesus is speaking of the End Times, of an eternal temple composed of stones no human hand has touched, and of those events that will immediately precede His glorious return.

Specifically, this is what He said: *Do you not see these things? Assuredly, I say to you, not one stone shall be left upon another, that shall not be thrown down (Matthew 24:2, NKJV).*

The disciples were shocked. Speechless! What was all this talk about the temple stones being thrown down into nothing more than a heap of so much rubble? That ended their pleasant afternoon, and it was not until evening that one of the disciples dared pursue the matter further: "What's wrong,

Introduction

Jesus? You're scaring us! What do you mean, these stones will be thrown down? How? When? What does the future hold? Tell us what to expect?"

Jesus responded with one of the great keys of all Christian theology. More than cryptically coded predictions about famines, wars, pestilence, and deceptions, Matthew, chapter 24 contained vital information for a pathway of safety through the End Times. In it, Jesus offered shocking, disturbing, yet also liberating and hopeful answers to our age-old questions—the same questions asked by the disciples so long ago: "What does the future hold? When will these things You have just described happen?"

The bombardment of technical terms surrounding the study of prophecy is often enough to drive many away in confusion. After all, it is confusing to try to understand all the techno-babble and keep straight the meaning of terms such as postmillennial, pretribulational, the Rapture, sea of glass, and so forth. It's like trying to learn "computerese"—RAM, megabyte, megahertz, gigabyte, hard drive, software, motherboard. All this End-Time lingo merely confuses the issue and makes it harder for the student of prophecy to come to any sort of spiritual enlightenment.

But please understand this one thing clearly: Jesus wants you to understand the foundations of biblical prophecy. He did not give you Matthew 24 to frighten you but to *enlighten* you and to help prepare you for what will surely come.

THE PURPOSE OF PROPHECY

In God's economy, nothing is wasted. There is a purpose for everything; for every season; for every passage of Scripture; for every Word that proceeds from the mouth of God, there is a corresponding purpose. And the purpose of prophecy is to warn, to admonish, to encourage, to correct, and to define the paths of God's people so they can walk circumspectly—correctly—in the light of God's Word.

The purpose of all prophecy is really very simple. First, *it declares God's absolute control.* At its deepest, most basic level, prophecy reminds us that God is in charge. Through the prophetic word, God is saying, "Remember that I am in control—not man, not nature, and certainly not politics. I want you to understand that regardless of the way circumstances may seem to dictate, things are not out of control. Satan is not winning; life is not chaos. I am in charge, and I know the end from the beginning."

Second, prophecy is meant *to prepare God's people to win in the future.* The purpose of prophecy is not to fill your mind with a bunch of numbers and names, dates and places, and empty promises that never seem to quite come to pass. The purpose of prophecy is to prepare you and inform you of what to do in order to win in the midst of every one of life's challenges. God is a practical God, and He wants His people to be ready, to have the advantage, to obtain insight prophetically, and to know what to do when the adversary hits.

Third, prophecy is meant *to give you a stable,*

Introduction

joyful, confident life. This is the good news about prophecy—understood and correctly applied, it will result in your leading a confident, prepared life and a Christian walk that will hold fast in the midst of chaos and turmoil.

So rather than to terrify, the purpose of prophecy is to edify. Rather than to confuse, the purpose of prophecy is to clarify. And Jesus very specifically outlines the things pertaining to the End Times in Matthew, chapter 24, while He clearly states that no man will know the exact moment of His coming. (If we were to know such things, why would anyone need faith?)

He is also speaking very specifically when He states, *See that ye be not troubled.* By this, we see these prophetic utterances are for our good—to hold us steady, to steer us around possible potholes in the way, to provide End-Time guideposts that will, in effect, anchor us against the shaking and quaking going on all around us. Jesus wants His children to be at peace—even in the midst of earthquakes, wars, rumors of wars . . . even in an atmosphere of betrayal and deception where men and women actually claim to be Christ come in His stead, Jesus wants His people to be at peace and rock-steady.

That's the good news.

The bad news is that accompanying any prophetic word, there is also always an element of danger—that it will be misunderstood, misappropriated, and that instead of clarifying what Christ is speaking to the church, it will confuse and even lead some astray.

That is the unfortunate dilemma of all prophecy.

The Dilemma of Prophecy

Jesus knew all about the dilemma of prophecy. That's why, loaded into His prophecy bomb, there were so many warnings as to its correct use and interpretation and even its timing.

Jesus is saying, "When you begin to see these things unfold, don't be troubled; this is merely the beginning of sorrows. After these things have been fulfilled and the gospel has been preached in every corner of the earth—then the end will come!"

The prophecy bomb, therefore, defuses every claim that specifically links a particular event to the end of time. It debunks every false Christ and phony prophet. It demystifies the End Times as it encourages us to look beyond these tumultuous events to His glorious return.

Yet we are flesh, and flesh inevitably wants its way. It wants to be right. It wants to fix things. It wants concrete—even immediate—answers. That's one reason why prophecy is so compelling. It strikes the same chord within each of us because each of us is interested in the future. Every stockbroker wants to know what the market holds. Every farmer wonders what the next crop will bring. Every mother worries about her children's futures as she packs them off to school, wondering, *Will my children be safe today? When they reach school, what kinds of dangerous influences will be waiting for them? When they finish school and start their lives as adults, will there be any moral fabric left within our disintegrating society?*

Introduction

Elderly people wonder if their futures are endangered by the flagging Social Security system and the rising interest worldwide in euthanasia—the cold-hearted annihilation of the weak, the elderly, and the infirm to make more room for the strong, the youthful, and the healthy. They worry about their futures in terms of safety as, frightened and often alone, they stare out their windows at crimes being committed in broad daylight. They lay awake nights, listening to the ominous wail of police and ambulance sirens.

Even our young people wonder if their futures are secure as they reach adulthood in an environment loaded with landmines such as drugs, AIDS, and killings over stupid things like designer tennis shoes or status bomber jackets. A current survey noted that 62 percent of grade-school children admitted they did not expect to live out their adult lives due to a nuclear holocaust or environmental catastrophe.

I recall vividly the day my own children asked me about AIDS. The eldest was no more than seven years old at the time. They asked me how a person got AIDS, and there I was—telling my young children about AIDS and how you get it, when I should have been telling them how to trade baseball cards or helping them with their spelling.

Prophecy is so compelling because it touches deep within us those secret needs and fears common to us all. We want to know the future, but it also makes us afraid. There is a sense of foreboding upon knowing the future: After all, what if the future is all bad? Where would the hope be then? And why would anyone need a measure of faith if the future was unfurled for us like a bright series of flags we simply follow to "pass go and collect two hundred dollars?" *Time* magazine calls this negativity about future events the "doom expectation," laying dormant down deep within each of us. It's that common fear of the unknown tnat all mankind carries as baggage from the Fall. We get anxious because we want to know the future, but we're frightened because we might not like what we learn. Surveys say people *fear* more than *embrace* the future. With that in mind, it's no wonder so many people read their daily horoscopes right after the front-page news. They want a peek into the future—just a little one. That's pretty harmless, isn't it?

But the Bible clearly warns against such dab- blings into the dark side of the prophetic. To be interested in prophecy from the biblical standpoint can be a blessing, but to wander down dark corri- dors of what is actually the occult is forbidden. And it carries with it a curse.

Jesus wanted to bless, not curse, His people by dropping the prophecy bomb. He wanted to encourage His people and also expose charla- tanism. He wanted to clearly demonstrate that prophecy, at its very core, is good news that pro- vides practical help for daily living. He was not trying to rain on the disciples' parade that long- ago day in Jerusalem. Nor is He trying to rain on ours today.

He was speaking out of His deep love—not just for the disciples who were His students and com- panions and friends, but for all mankind . . . so

Introduction

dear to Him that He was willing to die for the sum of all sin.

THE DANGERS OF PROPHECY

Jesus knew there were real dangers to prophecy. Yet He gave us the gift, fraught with its potential dangers, anyway. He gave it even knowing that misused or misunderstood, prophecy had the potential of confusing His people and leading some astray. Even knowing that lives could be damaged, perhaps even destroyed by the misuse of prophecy, Jesus gave us the gift.

Why did He do that?

For one reason, He knew there were more pluses than minuses to the gift of prophecy. For another, He knew that He is the Restorer—that He is able to fix what is broken in our lives. He knew that where there is head-knowledge and half-hearted commitment, He can provide *rhema*—the spiritual explosion of the knowledge of the Word of God inside our spirit-man—and total sold-out commitment to Jesus Christ as both Savior and Lord. Only Jesus can do that. Only Jesus can take a former prophecy freak like me and lead me back into the study of biblical prophecy from a balanced view, under the guidance and leadership of the Holy Spirit.

So just because there are dangers to out-of-balance prophetic teachings, we should not fear the Bible's prophetic passages, and we should certainly not fear the End Times. After all, the glory that awaits God's people when the Lord returns cannot even be comprehended by mortal man. And that is a cause for great joy.

How can we reach this state of joy at the mere thought of Christ's return? We must allow the Holy Spirit to transform us from shallow, inch-deep spirituality to deep, 100 percent commitment to Christ. Shallow commitment has no staying power. It results in trying to serve God with our own human ability—rather than in Spirit and in truth. Serving God with our own ability just leads to confusion, weariness, hurt, burnout. But when we are transformed in our inner man by the Holy Spirit, we put off the old man and put on the new man. We become prepared spiritually to meet the Lord. And that is cause for great rejoicing.

However, the Bible says that not everyone who calls Jesus Lord will wind up in heaven. Why is that? Because we won't make it unless we have confessed Jesus as Lord and Savior. Doing religious things, going to church regularly, serving on the right committees, and being faithful to hold bake sales and car washes is not enough. Approximately two-thirds of those who attend church regularly, studies reveal, may not make it to heaven because they have a skewed view of what it takes to get there. They think they must work their way there and somehow qualify for the grace of God—which is His free gift to mankind.

All it takes is to be transformed by the miracle of conversion—when we admit to God we can't make it to heaven on our own and need Jesus to justify us, forgive us, cleanse us, and become our Savior and our Lord. As Savior, He will deliver us from sin; as Lord, He will lead us in our daily lives and bring us into the place of inward transformation.

It's simple, really; being spiritual-minded begins with making a public declaration of commitment to Jesus Christ. Something exciting happens when we do that one simple thing. In so doing, we are saying to the world—and before all heaven—"I am now committed to Christ. I will die to myself and live to Him. Now I am risen into new life through Him."

And so begins your spiritual walk. Dare to be spiritual! Dare to take a different path! Dare to study biblical prophecy, and pray for the Lord to give you insight and understanding into the Word as it pertains to the End Times! Dare to grow deep in the wisdom and knowledge of God and to learn, then follow His path for your life. Dare to be sold out to Jesus! Dare to be His and His alone!

It's not always easy, and it's not always safe. Jesus said it would be so. But you must develop a balanced view of spirituality. Don't be surprised nor dismayed by the battles you face, because if you are not fighting spiritual battles, there may be something wrong. As far as I have observed, those who serve God suffer persecution and spiritual warfare as a matter of course. Christianity is wonderful, but it's no Disney World. So don't seek shortcuts or go hopping from one false prophet to the next to "get a word" from God. If He has a prophetic word for your life, He'll see that you get it; just let Him send it to you supernaturally as He chooses, and you'll be able to trust its accuracy.

Being truly spiritual is also admitting that everything about the Christian life isn't roses; sometimes there are battles that we need help in fighting if we are to win. Real Christians don't have to pretend everything is sweetness and light. They don't have to put up a big front. Paul the Apostle admitted his needs and shared his battles with others. Remember, you are not alone! We're all in the same boat and headed for the same destination—heaven!

Prophecy provides practical help to strengthen us in difficult times. It is both a gift and a weapon in the hands of God's people to help them win the intense spiritual battles that Jesus said would accompany the End Times. May the contents of this book help you to better understand and apply End-Time prophetic scripture as you fight the good fight in the days ahead.

1

SIGNS IN THE EARTH

An overwhelming *upheaval in the earth* marks the first great event of the future. According to Matthew 24:6–8, this onslaught of global disaster may be categorized in four ways—famines, pestilences, earthquakes, and wars. Jesus said, "And you will hear of wars and rumors of wars. See that you are not troubled; for all these things must come to pass, but the end is not yet. For nation will rise against nation, and kingdom against kingdom. And there will be famines, pestilences, and earthquakes in various places. All these are the beginning of sorrows" (NKJV).

THE NEXT 7 GREAT EVENTS OF THE FUTURE

Jesus said these signs in the earth would herald His coming. He said the earth would actually groan and travail until that time. He said there would be *earthquakes* (and other natural disasters, such as floods, volcanic eruptions, and violent, unusual, unpredictable weather patterns), *famine, pestilence, wars, and rumors of wars.* A case could even be made that all these things are happening on earth right now. They are. And they will continue. But the end is not yet.

These four dramatic, heart-wrenching events strike terror in us more than any of the other signs associated with the End Times because few things pierce our hearts more than the possibility of sudden, unexpected disaster. These are events over which we can exert no control—things that come upon us as if from nowhere. The devastation is swift. The destruction seems to follow no rhyme or reason, and often even the most elaborate protections against the inevitable prove to be no help when the crisis actually hits. Buildings still topple when the earthquake comes regardless of how "quake-proof" the builders claimed the design to be. Floods still wipe out entire counties—crops, houses, and all—despite the latest state-of-the-art dikes and levies. Viruses still attack for which there are no known cures in spite of the latest scientific anti-viral breakthroughs.

These signs are simply to tell us that the end is near. They help us to know the season we are in. They help us to walk circumspectly, knowing that Jesus is coming soon, so we will lead spiritually prepared lives—lives full of hope and victory, strength and joy. There is, after all, an awesomeness about living in the End Times. We are the generation who will see great things—signs in the earth and wonders associated with the glorious return of Christ.

There are always those who will argue that there have always been these things present on earth—there have always been earthquakes and floods, famine and pestilence, wars and rumors of wars. The answer to these naysayers is, "Yes—you're right; but never in history have these things occurred on such a large scale, or so frequently."

Jesus said these things would occur as signs in the earth to herald the End Times. But He meant for them to point the way to safety and success, not to terrify or offer up a snare. Still, it's easy to ignore or underestimate these signs. After all, we have grown accustomed to the bad news associated with devastation and loss, destruction and even death. How can we possibly associate spiritual significance to that which some claim are merely random happenings beyond all explanation or predictability?

FAMINE

Jesus said we would recognize the end was near when the famine began. And that time has come. Yes, it's true—famine has always been present somewhere on the planet. But famine has now become a problem that is global in proportion.

According to *Science* magazine, the population in 70 percent of the world's developing countries is outstripping their gains in food production. Paul Ehrlich, the secular "doomsday scientist," says, "For the first time in modern history, absolute global food deficits are present." According to one study by the United Nations Population Fund, the amount of land devoted to agricultural pursuits is decreasing rapidly, while new deserts are growing at the rate of 14.8 million acres per year. In addition, 26 billion acres of topsoil are lost per year, and 27 million acres of oxygen-producing rain forest disappear every year.

While the earth itself seems to be decreasing, the world's population is booming. One hundred million new people are added to the planet annually, and at the current rate, it means a billion will be added each decade. Of those, 786 million—or one out of six—will suffer from acute or chronic hunger at some point during their lives. A billion more face serious malnutrition, as in the case of victims of widespread famine in the African nation of Somalia:

> *Muslim Aden stands by the tiny grave, gently cradling the bundle of rags that holds the emaciated remains of her seven-year-old son. A few days earlier she buried her daughter who died of starvation, and before that her mother. Almost everyone from her village is dead. She says she has no more tears left. Welcome to Somalia, where strife and famine have claimed the lives of 350,000—most of them children.*

Two billion of earth's 5.5 billion people are

malnourished in some way, according to the United Nations' food and agricultural organization. The thought of even one billion hungry people is hard to comprehend for most of us. Yet the danger level of the world's food supply in relationship to its burgeoning population is so high that unless something happens, the end is closer than we would like to admit.

> *The distant sound you hear while you stand comfortably on the platform waiting for your train is not the oncoming train, but the sound of banging, empty rice bowls from one-third of mankind who are approaching starvation.*

Don't think this scenario couldn't happen in America, the land of plenty with its fields of amber grain. The U.S. Department of Agriculture says that America is merely one year of failed crops away from hunger, as our nation's food reserves continually diminish in proportion to its population. America's food reserves are the lowest since the Dust Bowl days. That means if for just one year the nation's crops do not succeed, America too will face extremely critical shortages to its food supply.

In addition, America's topsoil is nearly gone in some areas of the heartland. Gone are the days when pioneers of the United States and Canada found six to ten feet of rich topsoil that had been fallow for more than a thousand years. According to a recent survey, soil erosion has dropped that figure down to a scant three to five inches of topsoil, on average, throughout North America.

There is also great hunger to be found in the midst of prosperity. It's hard for us to imagine, but even in America, there is hunger. It happens! I have actually asked peeked-looking teenagers, "What's up? You look miserable!" only to be told, "I haven't eaten for two days!" Yet these same teens presented an upscale appearance, wearing the latest styles—designer jeans and tennis shoes. The sad part is that there is no reason for such famine in the midst of plenty. It's just not necessary. It's a sign. It's a byproduct of the times we're living in, when people are living on maxed-out credit cards and spending what they've earned on things like hundred-dollar tennis shoes and the latest techno-toys instead of stocking adequate food in their pantries to provide for the physical well-being of their families.

It's sad, because these shortages are not necessary. It's sad, because we have the ability to produce enough food to feed everyone in America if we would only work together unselfishly. We waste enough food to feed millions.

Yet beyond all those impersonal clouds of poor planning and the impending doom of floods and crop-ruining cold fronts, there is the hand of the supernatural. Jesus said, *"When you begin to notice the threat of famine is on the increase, then you'll know that the end is near; it's not yet . . . but it's beginning."*

Signs in the Earth

PESTILENCE

The second sign is pestilence. Webster's Dictionary defines *pestilence* as "a contagious or infectious, epidemic disease that is virulent and devastating in the destruction of life and injury to society." Have we not seen an increase in pestilence on planet earth? God uses another term as well for *pestilence,* and that word is *plague*—"an unsolvable killer or tormentor." God sent ten plagues upon Egypt to get the people's attention before He delivered the Israelites, and the Bible clearly states that once again, He will use plagues—viruses and bugs—to get our attention regarding spiritual things.

Viruses and bugs have been around virtually forever. But then something new began to develop—sickness for which there was no known cure took on global, epidemic proportions with the onslaught of AIDS and other killer-viruses. What could these new plagues signify if not the end of time?

Every few years dozens of new diseases manifest on earth that are beyond our human ability to cure. Twenty years ago, for instance, whoever heard of toxic shock syndrome, Lyme disease, Legionnaires' disease, or for that matter, AIDS? Yet these killers seemed to come from out of nowhere to become household names—dreaded and feared. The World Health Organization predicts that by the year 2000, approximately forty million people will be infected annually by the AIDS virus. The *Washington Post* states that already there are more than fifteen million AIDS victims worldwide. The Center for Disease Control and Prevention in Atlanta has published that the number of persons actually infected with the HIV virus in some areas is at least a hundred times greater than previously reported. AIDS is no longer the disease of homosexuals; it is predicted that in the next decade 80 percent of all AIDS cases will be spread by heterosexual women. That's one reason why I believe ministers will have an easier time preaching sexual abstinence—it is virtually the *only* antidote against the spread of AIDS that works.

In addition to these killer viruses, there is a new development in regard to existing viruses that have become so common we no longer fear them. Some of the bugs that have been around for so long have become suddenly resistant to antibiotics. There are also "mystery strains" that respond to no known treatment, and appear, then disappear once more quickly, unexpectedly. In America alone, more than fifteen sexually transmitted diseases are listed as incurable yet not always fatal.

Super-bugs, from killer bees to toxic ants, can no longer be controlled by powerful insecticides. In fact, many of these new super-bugs seem to scoff at what we humans spray at them. Super-rodents are also multiplying in population and effect—rats destroy more than one-third of all food produced on the planet.

Jesus told us to note these things—for when they begin to happen, the end is not yet. . . . *but it's near.*

Signs in the Earth

EARTHQUAKES

The third prophetic event Jesus mentioned as He dropped the prophecy bomb was earthquakes. There is something about such a cataclysmic event that sends shivers up the spine of even the most rock-solid believer. The very idea of experiencing an earthquake and the devastation accompanied by it that impacts all people deep within. Millions of Americans sat glued to their television sets as the devastation of the 1989 San Francisco earthquake unfolded before their eyes. Yet cataclysmic events are a part of the prophetic landscape, and again and again they crop up in Scripture, as in Acts 2:20:

The sun will be turned to darkness and the moon to blood before the coming of the great and glorious day of the Lord.

We don't have to look any further back in history than to the eruption of Mt. St. Helens in the State of Washington to know that cataclysmic activity on earth—such as the eruption of a long-dormant volcano—can have an impact upon the heavens, including the weather, long after. When Mt. St. Helens blew, it sent tons of volcanic ash into the atmosphere—enough ash to cover Manhattan Island to a depth of four hundred feet if all that ash had landed in one place at once. The sun was obscured by an ashen haze for long months following the actual incident. That one blast is simply indicative to a small degree of the force that God will unleash upon the planet in these End Times. Imagine!

But earthquakes can be caused by more than mere tremors beneath the earth's crust. What about the kind that would be caused if a speeding extraterrestrial meteor came crashing down on us? A popular magazine described it thus:

It comes screaming out of the sky like the scud from hell, bigger than a mountain and packed with more energy than the world's entire nuclear arsenal. It hits the atmosphere at a hundred times the velocity of a speeding bullet, and less than a second later, smacks into the ground with an explosive force of a thousand million megatons of TNT. The shock wave from the crash landing, traveling twenty thousand miles an hour, levels everything within a hundred and fifty miles. Simultaneously, a plume of vaporized stone shoots up from the impact site blasting a hole through the atmosphere and venting hot debris. Nitrogen and oxygen in the atmosphere combine into nitric acid. Any surviving life gets pelted with a rain as caustic as the acid in a car battery.

That's what astronomer Henry Melosh of the University of Arizona calculates would happen if something with a width of just six miles fell from space and smacked into earth. He says it's what killed the dinosaurs. Science fiction or future fact? *Planet Earth 2000* by Hal Lindsey provides an update on earth's upheaval from the Geological

Signs in the Earth

Survey in Boulder, Colorado. He begins with noting that between 1890 and 1899, only one "killer" quake occurred anywhere in the world measuring greater than 6.0 on the Richter scale. But beginning in 1900, all that changed.

- From 1900 to 1910, there were three.
- From 1910 to 1920, there were two.
- From 1920 to 1930, there were two.
- From 1930 to 1940, there were five.
- From 1940 to 1950, there were four.
- From 1950 to 1960, there were nine.
- From 1960 to 1970, there were thirteen.
- From 1970 to 1979, there were *fifty-one*.
- From 1980 to 1989, there were *eighty-six*.
- From 1990 to 1994, there were *more than a hundred* quakes of greater than 6.0 intensity.
- In 1995, there were *forty-seven*.
- In 1996, there were *seventy-two*.

And these are the facts. Scientists are still looking for the "big one" to hit California, and anticipate that it will be greater than 8.0 on the Richter scale—more than eighty-five times greater than the 1989 quake that rocked the city of San Francisco.

The quake hit in San Francisco in 1993, and that year *Life* magazine's cover story for its year-in-retrospect issue carried this headline: "The Year of the Killer Weather; Why has Nature Gone Mad?" The article stated that the worst deluge in sixty years had left thousands in Nepal and millions in India and Bangladesh homeless. The story also reported that it rained hard enough in the Philippines during the summer of 1993 to set off long-dormant Mt. Pinatubo. Rainwater seeped into the lava flow, where it became superheated and exploded into deadly steam. And these were only a few of the natural disasters experienced globally during a record year of upheaval on planet earth. When you add global warming, the depletion of the ozone layer, El Niño, the water crisis, algae growth, and increased worldwide pollution of the air and water supply, it's no wonder our kids are scared of what tomorrow may bring.

The end is near . . . *but not yet. . . .*

WARS AND RUMORS OF WARS

Wars. We've always had them. How could something so indigenous to mankind be associated as a sign of the End Times? How, indeed? With World War III looming ominously at the edges of our thinking, the threat of war takes on a larger-than-life reality when you add in nuclear capabilities in the hands of Third World nations, political hotheads such as Saddam Hussein and Yasser Arafat, and the ever-changing political climate of supernations like Russia and China.

"The question of the end of the world and World War III is not *if,* but *when. . . .*" a *Time* magazine analysis of war in the twentieth century stated. Such a statement is frightening but understandable. Mankind has not been free from war since 1945. In fact, standing armies of the world today total thirty-two million soldiers. As many as 50 percent of the world's scientists spend their waking hours making bombs and sophisticated weaponry, according to the Club of Rome (a "think tank" of one-worlders). A current survey by the U.S. Arms Control and Disarmament Agency reported that global military spending tops 930 billion annually.

A 1975 meeting between scholars from MIT and Harvard University determined that "the probability of nuclear war before the year 2000 [is] 100 percent." In addition, there have been ninety-six serious nuclear accidents to date, according to the Center for Defense Information. The end is edging closer.

General Douglas MacArthur summed up the lessons of World War II, the war that claimed more than sixty million lives, thus: "We have one last chance. If we do not now devise some greater and more equitable system, Armageddon will be at the door. The problem is basically theological and involves a spiritual renewal and improvement of human character. It must be of the spirit if we are to save the flesh." How prophetic!

War may be inevitable, but its roots are irrational. No reasonable person would destroy everything in order to make conquests. No thinking, reasoning person would ever conclude that war is the best way to solve political differences. War is destruction beyond all comprehension; yet mankind seems bent on touching off another world war! To some degree, we may even create our own tribulation by our repeated attempts to live without God.

Jesus did not say that war would disappear;

rather, that wars and rumors of wars would increase. And so it is. Man will not make more peace, despite all the "love and peace and harmony" rhetoric. War—not peace—will mark mankind's final chapter as it plays out upon the stage of planet earth.

Behind these wars and rumors of war, the Bible says, is the great ongoing battle between God and Satan—good and evil. But remember—God is in control. These signs are simply to remind us that it's the beginning of the end. And it's not yet, but it's getting closer. . . .

WHAT THE SIGNS MEAN TO US

Now, listen to a word of advice: The world isn't going to be a very nice place as these signs intensify around us. Do you believe me when I say that? Nor will it be easy to live in these End Times. It will get rough, and I want you to know that. But I also want you to know who's in charge. His name is Jesus, and He's the One who warned us that these times were coming.

So why would He give us these signs? And further, what do they mean to us—His people? First of all, these signs are meant as a general wake-up call to a people bent on living without God (see Rom. 1). God has given to each of us a free will, and when we choose to live according to that free will—with no thought given to God and His perfect plan for our lives—we often create our own "monsters." We make miserable messes of our lives, and many times those messes spill over onto others' lives and mess them up too. God loves us, but when we harden our hearts toward Him and continually go our own way, we put ourselves in danger of His judgment. Not because He hates us, but because He loves us, God gave us such a "wake-up call." He wants to bring us back to Him. And so He sends us signs.

Second, He wants the world's attention. The world, so bent on amassing political power and using it to oppress entire nations, is still the world God created and the world He remains sovereign over. When we refuse to acknowledge God, then He will send some big event—often cataclysmic in nature—to remind us He's still God and still very much in charge. He understands perfectly that mankind is selfish and hard-hearted, and yet He wants to warn us through such signs in the earth before it is too late.

Why is it that people take little notice when God whispers? We are too many times more "mule" than "lamb," stubbornly asking to be hit over the head with God's messages when He would rather speak to us gently and lead us beside the still waters. God will take such stern measures not because we like to get hit but because we refuse the gentle leading of the Holy Spirit.

God calls the world to attention through the things it values most—security, stability, and satisfaction. Trouble in any one of these areas strikes at the heart of what we're about and endangers what we most crave. So when war or disease threaten, our frail fleshly source of security is exposed for what it really is—rickety and untrustworthy. We should know by now that Jesus Christ is our only legitimate source of security. But some of us never seem to quite learn that lesson.

So the signs come in the earth as God attempts to reach mankind with the truth . . . before the end comes.

Jesus is saying, "Only I can make you safe and secure."

But sometimes we still need that wake-up call. Bam! An earthquake hits. People who haven't prayed in years suddenly find prayer welling up within them, crying out for mercy and deliverance, salvation and help in the midst of disaster. As Christians, how must we respond as the world reels around us? With kindness. With love. With faith. With confidence, because we know who is really in charge. And His name is Jesus.

HOW TO REACT SPIRITUALLY

So what are we to do in the midst of all this turmoil and nearly inevitable natural disaster? First of all, don't panic! That was Jesus' word to His people: "See that ye be not troubled." The reason He dropped the prophecy bomb was to warn and prepare, not to terrify and destroy. Jesus wanted us to know these things were up ahead so we would not become dismayed and lose our way spiritually as the path became obscured by hardness.

Don't panic! Panic hits when we are not prepared, not paying attention to the signs along the way. It blindsides us when we're not ready and delivers a series of blows to the solar plexus of our spirituality so that if Jesus didn't help us to quickly recover our balance and vision, we'd be sidelined. Panic opens the door to defeat and discouragement.

When we're properly prepared—and we will be as we study and pray for insights into the Bible's prophetic passages—we'll successfully avoid the panic trap set to rob us of the ability to respond appropriately. When life turns upside down, when the world is falling apart, don't panic; remember, God is in control! It's not the end of the world; it's simply near. So be concerned, but don't lose it.

Jesus said we would be tempted to get all worked up when we see these things beginning to unfold on a grand global scale. He said, "You will hear of wars and rumors of wars, but see to it that you are not alarmed. Such things must happen, but the end is still to come" (Matt. 24:6).

Jesus warned us to stay cool because He knew our propensity for panic at bad news. If we get a headache, then it's got to be a brain tumor! If our big toe hurts, it must be rheumatoid arthritis! Everything is always doom and gloom and terrible beyond belief; it's human nature. All this reminds me of the story of Chicken Little. He was sure the sky was falling just because an acorn fell from the highest branches of a tree and conked him on the head. He felt the blow, looked skyward, and cried, "The sky is falling! The sky is falling!" Everyone got upset and overreacted. The sky wasn't falling—an acorn was.

And so it is with the enemy; he blows everything

out of proportion in his clever, continual attempts to get us to overreact. He wants us to become fearful and thus neutralize our faith. He wants us to be easily deceived and led astray by the panic created as we dwell on the negative realities of the times we live in. He wants us to move from crisis to crisis rather than from glory to glory.

If we panic, we lose control. If we panic, we lose perspective. If we panic, we become moved by our emotions and easily overwhelmed by the scope of what we see happening around us in the natural realm. Too much emphasis on the natural realm—a byproduct of this panic—causes us to lose our spiritual vision. The result? Chaos. Defeat. Depression. Wrong decisions.

Pessimism is panic in its earliest stages, and history proves that pessimism creates a lifestyle of overreaction. William Pitt, prime minister of England, said, "There is scarcely anything around but ruin and despair." Such a doom-and-gloom statement was the byproduct of his pessimistic worldview. Disraeli, the great prime minister of France during the Napoleonic reign, said in 1849, "In industry, commerce, and agriculture, there is no hope." Shortly before his death in 1851, England's Duke of Wellington stated, "I thank God that I will be spared from seeing the consumption of ruin that is gathering around." These men missed many great things because of their despairing outlook on life.

One of the greatest attacks against believers in the days ahead will be panic, so don't treat this issue lightly. Stop looking at circumstances, because these will inevitably look bad—worse, in fact, than is actually the case. When prayer enters in, God changes things—even the most hopeless situation. He's in charge! You'll be tempted to handle things on your own rather than giving God a chance, but don't miss your miracle! Instead of overreacting, don't panic—pray, and see what God will do!

Each of us secretly battles fear and panic. Regardless of how spiritual we may seem on the outside, inside these battles rage on as we face the temptation to expect the worst—when actually God has a plan to take us by a way that we know not. These are temporary situations at best, and all play a part in God's plan.

Many times during His earthly ministry, Jesus told the disciples not to worry . . . to be at peace. "Peace I leave with you; my peace I give you. I do not give to you as the world gives. Do not let your heart be troubled and do not be afraid" (John 14:27). In moments of panic, He came to His disciples and spoke peace and encouragement. When, for example, He came to them on the water, He said, "It is I; don't be afraid" (John 6:20). Again, at the Resurrection, He spoke peace. Throughout Scripture, He says again and again, "Don't panic! Don't lose it! Trust in Me!"

Psalm 91 contains a message of peace and safety in the midst of trouble.

> *He who dwells in the shelter of the Most High will rest in the shadow of the Almighty. I will say of the Lord, "He is my refuge and my fortress, my God, in whom I trust." Surely he will save you from the fowler's snare and from the deadly*

pestilence. He will cover you with his feathers, and under his wings you will find refuge; his faithfulness will be your shield and rampart. You will not fear the terror of night, nor the arrow that flies by day, nor the pestilence that stalks in the darkness, nor the plague that destroys at midday. A thousand may fall at your side, ten thousand at your right hand, but it will not come near you. You will only observe with your eyes and see the punishment of the wicked. If you make the Most High your dwelling—even the Lord, who is my refuge—then no harm will befall you, no disaster will come near your tent.

—Psalm 91:1–10

Jesus is calling us to make a conscious decision to guard our hearts and lives against fear and pessimism. We must make the decision to trust Him in the midst of each circumstance and not panic. We must stay cool and refuse to lose it, when everyone around us—even believers—is losing it. We must not get sucked under by the emotional tide. Remember—God is in control, and this is not the end. . . . only the beginning of the end.

Stay focused! Too many times in the midst of pressure, we allow the world and its fears to make our decisions for us—when it's God who holds the key. The best way to keep fear from dominating is to stay focused with our eyes fixed firmly on Christ, who is our hope of glory (Col. 1:27). Jesus is saying, even today, "Fix your eyes on Me!

Signs in the Earth

Don't let the enemy rob you of your spiritual focus!"

So the temptation is to respond to the first of these seven great events with fear and anxiety. Jesus is saying, "Don't do that! Don't panic! Stay focused! Fix your eyes on Me, because only I can keep you from falling. Don't let the enemy distract you from My goal for your life!"

In life, you will face many crises. The enemy wants to send many crises your way in his ongoing attempts to distract you and infect you with a crisis mentality that keeps you off center with constant pressures. See that you don't lose your focus in times of pressure because it is your spiritual focus that contains the key to God's way out of each of these seemingly impossible circumstances. The enemy wants you to spin your wheels, spending hour after hour mulling over those things you have no power to change. Fix your eyes on Jesus, and He will make a way of escape for you.

If you begin to respond to the urgent rather than to the important in your life, you will soon find that you are living an emotion-driven life rather than a spirit-directed one. When you are emotions-driven, you are problem-conscious. You are sidetracked. Your power is reduced, and your faith is neutralized. You will not accomplish the things God wants you to accomplish.

In the John Bunyan classic, *Pilgrim's Progress,* Pilgrim got sidetracked from his spiritual quest and almost missed his true destiny—the will of God. Pilgrim's journey provides a good analogy for us today when so many distractions are pulling at us and vying for our attention. Stay focused! Don't be distracted! God is in control!

Jesus, too, was tempted to get involved with worldly events and political debates. He chose to stay focused on the will of the Father. He did not heal every sick person. He did not write a single book. He did not build a temple, and He occupied no actual earthly throne. He did not run for office and had no home of His own. Why? Because He stayed focused on the task at hand—Calvary and the salvation of mankind.

Guarding against life's distractions becomes a kind of warfare in the spirit realm. When we burn up time worrying about the things we cannot change, we lose both credibility and power. We fail to use what time and energy we have to accomplish the things we *do* have the power to change. Power comes into our lives when we stay within the sphere of our influence. Here, we say, "Jesus, I can't control the world, but I can do what You have called me to do! You are in charge, so help me to work for You while You take care of the rest!" When we move beyond that frame of mind, we become powerless.

Jesus at no time states that the non-spiritual things in life are of no value. What He does state is that these events should not control us or deter us from pressing through to the spiritual goal set before us—which is to win souls and work to advance His kingdom during our time on earth.

So don't quit. Don't panic. Don't lose your focus. The end is near . . . but it's not yet.

There are six more events to unfold—including what I call "the ultimate prophecy bomb," the recognition of Israel as the forgotten key to all biblical prophecy!

2

RECOGNITION OF ISRAEL AS THE FORGOTTEN KEY TO END-TIME PROPHECY

I *call the establishment of the State of Israel* "the ultimate prophecy bomb," because when Israel became a legitimate state in the eyes of the world in May 1948, that single, seemingly isolated incident started the prophetic timeclock ticking down toward the "zero hour" and the end of time. This one event, so loaded with destiny, touched off a whole series of other, related future events. Some of these we have watched unfold. Some are yet to come. But the key to understanding all biblical prophecy pertaining to the End Times clearly seems to be Israel, and the world's recognition of its sovereignty in the eyes of God.

Nowhere on earth does so much turmoil swirl and writhe. Nowhere are so many seething emotions churning so close to the surface, ready at any moment to erupt in full-blown global warfare. Nowhere do the roots of cultural hatred go down so deep or surface so irrationally as in Israel—the biblical Promised Land of the Jewish people and the seat of three faiths. Jews, Muslims, and Christians all lay spiritual claim to the land of Israel. But to the Jews only, it was promised.

And to Israel, from all four corners of the globe, the Jews have returned. In the last two decades, long-dispersed Jews have flocked from foreign soil back to Israel, in fulfillment of more age-old scripture. And we must not overlook the fact that in continuing to watch what happens in the land of Israel, we are seeing the key slowly begin to turn, unlocking the final prophetic timetable on planet Earth.

PEACE WHEN THERE IS NO PEACE

Pacts and peace talks, summits, and shuttle diplomacy can all end just one way—God's way—as time ticks on, toward that one final moment when it runs out . . . and Jesus gloriously returns to set His foot on the Mount of Olives. That's where the Bible says He will first step, when the fullness of time has been accomplished and the Lord arrives to begin His thousand-year earthly reign. Until that day, Israel and the Middle East are "ground zero" in terms of biblical prophecy. As the world anxiously watches and awaits the inevitable—war between Israel and the rest of the world's governments—Israel will continue to be both the center of political upheaval and the key to End-Time prophecy.

Temporal things may change, and every other circumstance may vary. But you can bank on the fact that Israel will play an increasingly strategic role in the End-Time prophetic landscape. For the Bible says the temple that was built twice, and twice toppled, will be rebuilt again—and indeed the plans are already being laid—only this time it will be the site where the Antichrist sets himself up as lord over mankind. Then all Israel will be horribly persecuted, and the ones who heed the voice of God will flee to the mountains where He will protect them. Then Christ will come and reveal Himself to the Jews in the desert, and those who pierced Him will receive Him.

"But," you may say, "What does any of this have to do with *us*—with *Christians?*" Plenty! You cannot understand prophetic scripture unless you also understand the significance of events both ancient and current in Israel and the Middle East. It's no new revelation, but again I remind—Jesus was a Jew. He was born not in America but in Israel. That is His homeland. It's where He will return. It's where He will rule once His millennial reign begins on earth.

But we are tempted to think of everything about the End Times in terms of just what it may mean to us—Christians, Americans mostly. And if we're not careful, we'll begin to think that *we* are the center of End-Time prophecy—not Israel and the

Jewish people. That's not so. We are part of it, granted. But we are not the center. We are not "ground zero." *Israel is.*

THE ULTIMATE PROPHECY BOMB

The ultimate prophecy bomb, as I like to call it, was dropped by God at midnight on May 14, 1948, when Israel miraculously sprang into being as a nation. A few strokes of the pen, and what Jews everywhere had been waiting for for centuries became a reality. They again had a nation to call their own, just as God had promised long ago. Until that moment, the Jews had been scattered to the four corners of the world—in complete accordance with ancient prophecies, I might add. Those few remaining Jews in Europe had long lived in fear and the danger of total annihilation. Hitler's "final solution" had nearly succeeded, and six million Jews were wiped out in Germany, Poland, France, and other parts of Europe where the Jews were trodden down by the dreaded "storm troopers."

Suddenly, out of nowhere, Israel becomes a nation. Jews begin to flock there from all parts of the globe. What's more, the little nation begins to develop a very large roar.

The End-Time clock begins to tick, counting down the precious little time left between the formation of the State of Israel . . . and Christ's imminent return.

Ahead there would be struggles between God and Satan, good and evil, Christ and the Antichrist,

Israel and every other country on earth. For the Bible states that the day will come when all nations turn against small Israel, leaving her alone to stand against the wiles of the Antichrist who defiles the rebuilt temple and attempts to oppress the entire world's population.

Who would've believed forty . . . thirty . . . even twenty years ago that Israel would become, not simply a nation recognized by all the other nations of the world but a viable force in terms of world politics? Who would have believed that Israel would rapidly build a stable economy, learn to irrigate its vast desert lands, and thereby trigger fulfillment of another scriptural prophecy—that barren Israel's deserts would one day "blossom as the rose" (Isa. 35:1, KJV)? Yet small Israel continues to confound those who may be deceived by her meager size and relative youth as a nation. She has been a nation—in God's sight, anyway—for four thousand years, and the Jews have always belonged there; they were simply a rebellious people, so they spent a long time in exile. Ask any Jew, and you'll hear the same answer. Israel *belongs* to the Jews—the descendants of Abraham.

THE LAND OF ABRAHAM AND ISAAC

In 3000 B.C., God came to Abraham in a vision and told him, "I want to make you a father of many nations." Now, that was a pretty tall order, since at that time Abraham was a nobody named Abram, living in exile in nearby Mesopotamia, and a very old man with no children of his own. Yet here is God, saying to Abram, "Follow Me. And if you choose to follow Me, I will make a covenant with you and you will become a father of many nations." Now, even Abram knew that in order to become a father of many nations, he would first, at the very least, have to father at least one son.

In Genesis, chapter 12, the Lord says to Abram, "Leave your country, your people and your father's household and go to the land I will show you. I will make you into a great nation and I will bless you; I will make your name great, and you will be a blessing. I will bless those who bless you, and whoever curses you I will curse; and all peoples on earth will be blessed through you" (vv. 1–3).

So Abram follows God, and he is indeed blessed. He merely obeys, having no clue as to why God has called him and not some other member of his family. Perhaps there was no reason for God to call Abram other than the fact that he was a man who knew a little something about faith. He followed God, blindly by faith, just because God said, "Follow!"

The key word here is *covenant*. Abram realized that to make a covenant with someone was one of the most powerful, binding forms of agreement known to man. To come into covenant with someone was to promise to fulfill, no matter the cost, the exact terms of the covenant agreement to the absolute fullest degree. When God made His covenant with Abram, he knew that the Lord would fulfill His end of the promise—no matter what.

But the promise of God—a son, from which would spring mighty nations—did not come quickly. Abram—now Abraham—became even older, as did his wife, Sarah. Both became weary in the waiting. And when no son came, Sarah went to her servant-girl Hagar to arrange Plan *B*.

"Now, go into Abraham and bear him a son," Sarah ordered Hagar. So the beautiful servant-girl of Egyptian origin obeyed, conceived, and bore a son, Ishmael. But Ishmael was not the son God promised.

Anyone who has ever waited on God to perform His word of promise will understand eventually the temptation that comes with the waiting—the temptation to take things into one's own hands and "help God out." That's all Abraham and Sarah did, they "helped God out;" and when Hagar bore a son by Abraham, trouble soon erupted—trouble that simmers and seethes yet today among the children of Ishmael—the Arab nations of the world.

Abraham knew that God was a man of His word; yet, persuaded by Sarah, he nevertheless got ahead of God and bore—not a son of the Spirit, but a son of the flesh—Ishmael, using his free will to make the covenant-promise of God a reality. He had, after all, made a pact with God— so God was bound by His own Word to fulfill His promise to Abraham. Only strife and enmity resulted of Abraham and Sarah taking this one thing into their own hands, and even Sarah began to resent both Hagar and the son she bore. Finally, the only solution seemed to be to send the mother and son away.

Did Abraham forget that God could not lie? How was it that he convinced himself that God might send his son through Hagar and not Sarah? Finally, when child-bearing certainly seemed impossible ("I'm too old!" Sarah declared, and laughed), the Lord sent the blessing and opened childless Sarah's womb. She and Abraham conceived, and Isaac—the son of promise—was born. Through Isaac came the great nation of Israel.

Ever since, the descendants of Ishmael have been at odds with the children of Isaac. The roots of the hatred go down so deep, some can no longer remember exactly why it is that Arabs and Jews hate each other with such vitriolic fervor.

But stranger things than this unexplainable hatred would happen in the course of the drama that has been played out through history upon the stage of Israel—this curious land of promise.

"NOT ONE STONE HERE WILL BE LEFT ON ANOTHER!"

On a pleasant afternoon, during a casual stroll past the temple, Jesus drops the bomb:

> *"Do you see these things?" he asked. "I tell you the truth, not one stone here will be left on another; every one will be thrown down." As Jesus was sitting on the Mount of Olives, the disciples came to him privately. "Tell us," they said, "when will this happen, and what will be the sign of your coming and of the end of the age?"*
>
> —Matthew 24:2–3

Recognition of Israel . . .

When Jesus dropped the prophecy bomb that day during Passover, as He strolled past the temple surrounded by His disciples, it was a pretty difficult thing for the disciples to comprehend. After all, the first temple had stood four hundred years. This current one, even more glorious and elaborate, had been standing for nearly six hundred. A single one of its stones weighed several thousand tons, and this fabulous temple built by Solomon was considered one of the wonders of the world.

Not a single stone left standing?

Surely this could never be!

But Jesus could not lie—and sure enough, on May 10, A.D. 70, the largest Roman army ever assembled stormed into Jerusalem to do the unthinkable: annihilate the city and raze the temple to its foundations—a scant forty years after Jesus dropped "the prophecy bomb."

You may think this event occurred over some major political intrigue. However, you'd be wrong. It happened over a bird.

That's right—a bird. According to Dr. Gary Cohen, a Jewish historian, a riot broke out in the streets of Jerusalem in May of A.D. 66, and it was this internal strife—not an actual war—that led to the destruction of the temple. On the Sabbath day, some Greeks killed a bird perched atop an earthen vessel. The Jews who observed the episode became offended, interpreting the event as a "mock sacrifice" by a foolish and unclean people who meant to ridicule the Jews. A fight broke out that led to a riot. Pent-up racial animosity and cultural hatred heated up the conflict, and many Jews were killed. The Jewish leaders were angry over the incident and paid the Roman procurator, Gessius Florus, to protect the Jewish people. Gessius Florus was so angered at the embarrassment of this gesture that he fined the Jews seventeen gold talents.

These political twists and turns drove the Jewish zealots into a frenzied state, and they began to mock the Roman leader. Florus, by now enraged, ordered the Roman garrison to kill every Jew in sight. Three thousand six hundred Jews died over Florus' edict.

Jewish zealots rioted against the Roman authorities and seized control of lower Jerusalem and the temple. While the high priest pleaded for peace, the zealots responded by burning his house and branding him a traitor. The whole city of Jerusalem was now in chaos.

When the commander of the Roman garrison attempted to entreat the zealots to peace, the Jewish leaders came out of the temple, threw down their weapons as if in surrender, and proceeded to slaughter the Roman soldiers. News of the ambush raged through the streets of Jerusalem like wildfire. The news reached the Roman governor, Gallus, who committed his 12th Legion to march against Jerusalem and quell the riots. Six thousand of Rome's most battle-seasoned men marched down the coastal highway toward Jerusalem, while the Jews—filled with holy indignation and believing "God is for us"—ambushed these troops also, wiping out all six thousand men.

The Jews saw this second victory as the vindication of God; Rome saw it differently.

Recognition of Israel . . .

Emperor Nero was by now involved, and he announced his goals—to destroy the temple, plow the ground level, then sow the earth with the blood of its rebel-inhabitants. Nero dispatched retired General Vespasian to lead the vengeful crusade in January of A.D. 67. Vespasian successfully completed his mission, but only after trampling city after Jewish city in his path toward Jerusalem.

Meanwhile, the Jews had begun to kill each other as civil war erupted. The fighting was over who was more loyal, the followers of Moses or those of Jehovah. Tens of thousands of Jewish men died trying to protect their position on this small matter of dividing the Jewish law.

Josephus states that some of the Jews actually began to pray that Rome would come to save them from the zealots and the bloody civil war. Vespasian arrived at the walls of Jerusalem in A.D. 68, leading a massive army of fifteen Roman legions and the Praetorian guard, the crack troops of the Roman Empire. Then something incredible happened! Civil war broke out in Rome, and as the empire teetered on the brink of collapse, Nero was assassinated . . . and Vespasian became emperor. On receiving the news in Jerusalem, Vespasian returned to Rome and placed his son, Titus, in charge of finishing off the bloody business with the Jews.

It is on Passover—exactly forty years to the day after Jesus prophesied that the temple would be destroyed—that Titus and his mighty army would surround the city, trapping all of its inhabitants. Because it is Passover, nearly a million Jews had jammed into Jerusalem to observe the holy feasts. Instead of celebration, there was only suffering.

Food and water supplies were cut off, and tens of thousands of men, women, and children starved to death in the weeks to follow. The country was stripped of its trees within a twelve-mile radius as crude crucifixes were constructed by the Romans to put to death five hundred Jews a day after the manner of Jesus' agonizing death. The city walls were surrounded by such atrocities; yet, unbelievably, the Jews kept right on killing each other as the civil war continued to rage, even in the midst of such Roman persecutions. One of the Jewish factions started a fire that led to the destruction of reserves of corn that could have fed the city for years to come.

The death toll was over 1.1 million people by that time. And just as Jesus had prophesied—Solomon's temple was torn down stone by stone. The ground beneath it was plowed, just as Nero had ordered before his murder, and the blood of Jews soaked the land.

All because some Greeks killed a little bird with a stone on the Sabbath, angering some Jewish bystanders. God had performed His word.

A LAND OF SUFFERING

History tells us that Israel has suffered more than any other nation on earth. Why would this be so, if the Jews were indeed the apple of God's eye? Why would they be driven from their homeland? Forced to live as strangers in a foreign land? Persecuted again and again for their faith? Brutally killed by the millions at the hand of a madman? What does all this mean to us, as Christians?

Recognition of Israel . . .

History speaks from the pages of the Old Testament to teach us. God tells us about Israel so we can learn from this great nation. Israel holds the key both to the past and to the future. The Lord said we would know the season by the events occurring among the Jewish people:

When all these blessings and curses I have set before you come upon you and you take them to heart whenever the Lord your God disperses you among the nations, and when you and your children return to the Lord your God and obey him with all your heart and with all your soul according to everything I command you today, then the Lord your God will restore your fortunes and have compassion on you and gather you again from all the nations were he scattered you. Even if you have been banished to the most distant land under the heavens, from there the Lord your God will gather you and bring you back. He will bring you to the land that belonged to your fathers, and you will take possession of it. He will make you more prosperous and numerous than your fathers.

—Deuteronomy 30:1–5

For I will take you out of the nations; I will gather you from all the countries and bring you back into your own land.

—Ezekiel 36:24

They will fall by the sword and will be taken as prisoners to all the nations. Jerusalem will be trampled on by the Gentiles until the times of the Gentiles are fulfilled.

—Luke 21:24

Now learn this lesson from the fig tree: As soon as its twigs get tender and its leaves come out, you know that summer is near. Even so, when you see all these things, you know that it is near, right at the door. I tell you the truth, this generation will certainly now pass away until all these things have happened.

—Matthew 24:32–34

The return of the Jews to Palestine sent shock waves around the world. All attention was riveted there, as one report appearing in the *New York Times* on May 14, 1948, reveals:

TEL AVIV, PALESTINE—*The Jewish state, the world's newest sovereignty to be known as the State of Israel, came into being in Palestine at midnight upon termination of the British Mandate.*

Amazing! In one fell swoop a whole series of scriptures are fulfilled.

As generation after generation of Jews awaited these fulfillments of God's promises to them, here was a generation that was actually seeing them come to pass before their very eyes. And the world watched as the nations around the globe gave up their Jews—even those imprisoned and barred against their will from emigrating to Israel. In practically the twinkling of an eye, the deserts of Israel began to bloom with prosperous agricultural kibbutzes, where everything from lush tropical fruits to all kinds of flowers—including roses—flourished under the blessed hands of farmers who employed the latest technology to bring into being age-old biblical prophecy.

Again, the eyes of the world are fixed on Israel.

The lines are drawn.

Tempers again rage.

It is now both politically and economically advantageous to become "friends" with Israel, for there is oil there. There are technologies and minerals and trillions of dollars that flow through Israel that the world's powerbrokers would love to get their hands on.

Thus, it is again the age-old conflict between Abraham's two children—the descendants of Ishmael and the descendants of Isaac—brewing, but we now call it by another name. Now it is far more than a nation's birthright that is at stake. Now money and power and natural resources beyond belief stoke the fires of hatred and keep political intrigue at a fevered pitch in the land of Abraham's children.

AND THEN THE END WILL COME

Here is what the Bible says will happen in Israel in

the final seven years of time as we know it. The Bible calls this period of time the Tribulation. And during this period—

- The temple will be rebuilt at the midway point of the Tribulation.

- The Antichrist will set up one of his world headquarters there.

- The conflict will rage there between the Antichrist and children of God, and Israel will be at the heart of the conflict during the second half of this seven-year period.

- Israel will make a pact with the Antichrist in a last-ditch attempt to make peace.

- Russia and the Arab nations will attack Israel without warning in a great war the Bible calls the "war between Gog and Magog" (see Ezek. 38).

- The Antichrist will deceive everyone and set himself up as God, then try to destroy Israel as he oppresses the entire planet's population.

- God will miraculously protect "a remnant" (144,000 Jews who turn to Christ when He reveals Himself to them).

- Christ will return to Israel.

Can you see why Israel's role is so strategic to End-Time prophecy? It is a key that unlocks both past and future, and we can learn many priceless lessons as we study the Word as it pertains to Israel and the Jewish people.

Recognition of Israel . . .

WHAT ISRAEL CAN TEACH US ABOUT KEEPING OUR SPIRITUAL IDENTITY

I recall my first trip to Israel, and how ambivalent I was about going there. Here was the seat of biblical Christianity, and I could care less about seeing it for myself! But although I loved Bible prophecy, there was a piece of the prophetic puzzle that seemed to be missing in terms of my understanding. After my trip to Israel, it dawned on me that Israel was the missing puzzle piece! That's right—Israel was what had been missing! For some reason, I had failed to comprehend the spiritual significance to the serious-minded Christian of the place the Jews occupy—have always occupied—in the prophetic timetable. It began with the Jews, and so will it end with the Jews. They are God's chosen, favored people. They are God's beloved. The nation of Israel is the center of God's plan for this world, and Israel is certainly not to be forgotten.

Vital to an accurate understanding of End-Time events is this central idea of Israel as the key to all Bible prophecy! That is what was missing for me, and since God began to reveal these things to me, I can more aptly see the prophecies of the Bible as one seamless whole entity—a single strand woven from the opening of the Book of Genesis right through to the end of Revelation!

We must respect the Jews, not treat them with disdain. We must not hate them or reject them, as so many have done in Christ's name throughout history. We must acknowledge their position in the plan of God, as well as acknowledge that the Jewish people are deeply involved in End-Time events. The Jews have a powerful message for Christians; they witness to God's covenant-keeping love throughout history. Every great prophetic book in the Bible has Israel as its theme, as in this passage in the Book of Zechariah:

> *For thus saith the Lord of hosts; after the glory hath he sent me unto the nations which spoiled you: for he that toucheth you toucheth the apple of his eye.*
>
> —Zechariah 2:8, KJV

What will set the stage for the final chapter of earth history is the rebuilding of the temple on Jerusalem's temple mound. God will see that the temple is restored as a type of His restoration to the people of Israel. He will reach down to restore Israel when everyone and everything seems pitted against them and positioned to do them nothing but harm, just as Daniel prophesied centuries ago:

> *After the sixty-two "sevens," the Anointed One will be cut off and will have nothing. The people of the ruler who will come will destroy the city and the sanctuary. The end will come like a flood: War will continue until the end, and desolations have been decreed.*
>
> —Daniel 9:26

Here is the unbelievable! The rebuilt temple will

again be destroyed . . . and rebuilt once more. God judges His people, destroys His own house, then restores it as He restores His people when everyone else is against them! Where is the logic?

But then, there is no logic when we try to comprehend God's dealings throughout history with His chosen people. We can't use logic in determining why God chose Abraham to father those many nations; who knows why? Abraham didn't even know why! But Abraham nevertheless became the father of many nations, just as God had promised—and those nations sprang forth not from his "blood-line" but from his "faith-line." The New Testament admonishes us to walk as Abraham did—by faith. And if we do so, then we too shall be known as "the children of Abraham." What irony!

There is no logic in understanding how a Messiah to the Gentiles would spring forth from the Jewish people who first rejected, then crucified Him. And there is certainly no logic in the way that God continued to keep covenant with the Jews, even after they refused to receive their long-awaited and long-prophesied Messiah.

We Christians, too, are a covenant people, and as such, we can learn something about covenant-keeping from the Jewish people. After all, we get into Christianity the same way Abraham did—by covenant, by faith. We can learn something about spiritual community and identity by studying the Jews. As the Jews have done throughout history, and even against great odds and amid tremendous persecutions, we must learn to keep our spiritual identity and hold fast to it at any cost. We must learn spiritual tenacity. But we must learn from them how tragic it truly is to lose one's liberty in order to realize its value and importance.

Here was Israel—a godly nation—blessed of all the nations of the world but unable to retain that position. They faced enemies, fought battles, and won against great obstacles. They became great and built the greatest house of God the world has ever known; yet they lost everything because they neglected the foundations of their faith. They forgot God. They forgot that covenant relationship was a two-way relationship, and that their part was to be faithful to God and to His Word. When they became blessed, they failed the test of prosperity and freedom. The result was judgment, and judgment always begins in the house of God. "It is a fearful thing to fall into the hands of the living God" (Heb. 10:31, KJV).

There are great positives to be gained from the study of God's dealings with the Jewish people. There are also great dangers to heed. And American Christians in particular must heed them, for if ever there was a nation ripe for judgment, it is this nation. Billy Graham has stated, "If God does not soon judge America, then He will have to apologize to Sodom and Gomorrah." These are critical times for America, and her Christians must take seriously the call to prayer, repentance, and spiritual steadfastness.

So here are a few of the lessons from the Jewish people that will help us in our Christian walk during the End Times.

Recognition of Israel . . .

1. WE MUST NOT FORGET GOD.

We must pray continually for wisdom, humility, and daily dependence. We must seek Him in His courts, in prayer. We must not become too busy for Him once He begins to bless and promote us. The Israelites were greatly blessed but became so taken with their accomplishments and status that they forgot that it was God—not their own efforts—that had brought the blessing upon them.

2. WE MUST NOT FORGET OUR CHRISTIAN HERITAGE.

If we do, we shall surely go into spiritual captivity. That's what happened to Israel, and it's yet another warning we must heed.

3. WE MUST NOT FORGET TO TEACH OUR CHILDREN CHRISTIAN VALUES.

We must instruct our children as carefully as the Jews imparted their faith down through the generations to their children's children. We must see ourselves as God's people—as do the Jews.

4. WE MUST NOT NEGLECT HOLINESS.

We must be both loyal and pure and keep free of idolatry. If we do these things, God will bless us as He did the Jews. He will hold us steady through the storms of trials and tribulations if we walk in holiness and godly fear.

5. WE MUST NOT FORGET TO WALK IN LOVE AND UNITY.

The Romans who sought to subdue the rioting zealots knew that the secret would be to weaken them from within. "Why fight against them when they are killing each other?" the Roman generals reasoned. "Let them weaken themselves, and then we will march into their city!" Luke 11:17 states: "Jesus knew their thoughts and said to them: 'Any kingdom divided against itself will be ruined, and a house divided against itself will fall.'" Divided, we fall; united, we stand. And the key to unity is love. "Finally, all of you, live in harmony with one another; be sympathetic, love as brothers, be compassionate and humble. Do not repay evil with evil or insult with insult, but with blessing, because to this you were called so that you may inherit a blessing. For, whoever would love life and see good days must keep his tongue from evil and his lips from deceitful speech. He must turn from evil and do good; he must seek peace and pursue it" (1 Pet. 3:8–11).

6. WE MUST REMEMBER THAT AS CHRISTIANS, WE ARE FAMILY.

The Jews had great regard for family ties. As Christians, we belong to the family of God. "For he himself is our peace, who has made the two one and has destroyed the barrier, the dividing wall of hostility" (Eph. 2:14). The greatest power of Christianity is the power of love. Jesus said, "Love one another. As I have loved you, so you must love one another" (John 14:34). "Anyone who claims to be in the light but hates his brother is still in the darkness. Whoever loves his brother lives in the light, and there is nothing in him to make him stumble. But whoever hates his brother is in the darkness and walks around in the darkness; he does not know where he is going, because the darkness has blinded him" (1 John 2:9–11). We must love not only our enemies but each other because we are family. Let us learn from Israel how to love each other as family.

7. WE MUST REMEMBER THAT ANYTHING WORTH HAVING IS WORTH FIGHTING FOR.

We must fight for the right things, not just to be interpreted as right. The two factions who fought one another in Jerusalem in A.D. 68 each thought themselves right in their own sight. They slaughtered each other and went into Roman captivity. We must "major on the majors, and be tolerant of the minors." We must fight the right battles, at the right time, for the right reasons, with the right weapons—and the greatest of all weapons is love. Remember, this world is going to be an increasingly ugly place to be. People will become more and more unthankful, unholy, blasphemous, lovers of pleasure, unforgiving, slanderous—and there will be great reason for us to become offended and hurt. We must not be sucked downward by the mean-spirited pull of this world. We must reject the temptation to hurt back. We must respond with graciousness. "You have heard that it was said, 'Love your neighbor and hate your enemy.' But I tell you: Love your enemies and pray for those who persecute you, that you may be sons of your Father in heaven" (Matt. 5:43–48). We must love our enemies and show kindness without compromising essential doctrines.

8. WE MUST REMEMBER TO SEE THE WORLD THROUGH EYES OF FAITH.

Year after year, on Passover, the Jewish Patriarch would raise his glass in a toast that always ended with, "Next year in Jerusalem!" What a faith-loaded statement! And finally, it was so. One of the most powerful gifts of Christ was His faith in our potential in Him! Faith is still one of the most powerful weapons in a believer's arsenal. And at no time in history will faith be as important as it is in the End Times.

It is imperative that we see through eyes of faith as Abraham did. "Against all hope, Abraham in hope believed and so became the father of many nations, just as it had been said to him, 'So shall your offspring be.' Without weakening in his faith, he faced the fact that his body was as good as dead. . . . Yet he did not waver through unbelief regarding the promise of God, but was strengthened in his faith and gave glory to God, being fully persuaded that God had power to do what he had promised" (Rom. 4:18–22). Blessings come to those who see life, themselves, and each other as God sees—through eyes of faith. To see by faith is to see possibility in the midst of failure, miracle in the midst of pain, reality beyond possibility, light at the end of the tunnel.

9. *We must take the time to become grounded in the Word.*

The Jews prospered as long as they paid attention to the foundations of their faith. When they drifted from those foundations, judgment resulted. No one can build our "spiritual houses" for us; we are each responsible for our own spiritual dwelling, for our own spiritual development. "Therefore everyone who hears these words of mine and puts them into practice is like a wise man who built his house on the rock. The rain came down, the streams rose, and the winds blew and beat against that house; yet it did not fall, because it had its foundation on the rock. But everyone who hears these words of mine and does not put them into practice is like a foolish man who built his house on sand. The rain came down, the streams rose, and the winds blew and beat against that house, and it fell with a great crash" (Matt. 7:24–27).

10. *We must not break covenant with Christ.*

There will be storms, pressures, and challenges in these End Times—enough to try even the most committed believers. But God is calling us to stand fast in faith, trusting Christ as we were changed by the trials and liberated by the pressures to become known as a people of faith . . . like the Jews. Christ is the One who will keep us even in the most severe trials, even in the most violent storms, even in the midst of great darkness.

THE NEXT 7 GREAT EVENTS OF THE FUTURE

LIGHT AT THE END OF THE TUNNEL

There are dark days ahead; the Bible tells us this is so. But after the darkness comes the light! We can joyfully anticipate the Rapture and Christ's return, and the light that these events will bring to drive away the darkness. One day soon our hearts will again be made whole; our tears will be wiped away.

God has called us to be liberated from darkness and transformed by the marvelous light of Christ: "In Him was life, and the life was the light of men" (John 1:4, KJV). Even in the darkest hour, He is there to light our way and keep the terms of our covenant with Him. If we could only see beyond the veil into His miracle-working power! He has miracles yet to perform in this final hour, and we'll see signs and wonders, I am convinced, as at no other time in history. In Haggai, we are told: "The glory of this present house will be greater than the glory of the former house" (Hag. 2:9). We are living in that hour! We are the ones who will watch as the final chapter of Earth's history is being written. And much of it is being written in Israel in the Middle East.

Meantime, as we recognize Israel as the key to all Bible prophecy, we will inevitably come to the realization that in watching what is happening in Israel, we are actually witnessing End-Time events unfold. . . . And the next event is the rise of "Mystery Babylon."

3

THE RISE OF "MYSTERY BABYLON"

Why so much emphasis on "Mystery Babylon," as it is called in Revelation 17:5? As any good "prophecy freak" will tell you, "Mystery Babylon" is packed with prophetic significance. But what most don't know is that Babylon is mentioned two hundred times from Genesis to Revelation. It's as ancient as time itself. I could take all day, going off in any one of a number of directions in the examination of this topic. But as a believer in search of the more balanced approach to prophetic truths, I would like to caution against going to extremes when in search of insight and understanding about this most interesting of End-Time phenomena.

You've heard of Babel—that city built by Nimrod in the land of Shinar, where the "Tower of Babel" got its name (see Gen. 10:9–11, KJV). There's more to the story of the Tower of Babel than meets the eye; it's a classic war story—the story of man's attempt to engage God in a clash of authority. It's the tale of man's earliest effort to take the place of God—a form of rebellion. "Come, let us build ourselves a city, with a tower that reaches to the heavens, so that we may make a name for ourselves and not be scattered over the face of the whole earth" (Gen. 11:4).

From Babel came Babylon, a city basking in the reflection of the glory of its own pride rather than the glory of God. The people of Babylon, the Babylonians, were not shy about telling the world what they wanted. They wanted to control their own destinies. They wanted to be unified, amassing power for themselves to wield against their enemies. They wanted power in place of God, control of their own destinies. Their error was not in wanting to make something of themselves; it was in trying to do it on their own. The issue was authority; the Babylonians wanted no one in charge of them. Here was the message of Babylon: "I want self-sufficiency—my will, not God's for my life."

These are things most people don't realize about "Mystery Babylon." They hear the term and immediately think of Armageddon, 666, and the Antichrist.

So before we even get off on subjects like the mark of the beast and the current wave of speculation about whether or not the Antichrist is alive and well and living on the earth today, let's examine the roots of "Mystery Babylon" and see what we may learn about its influence on today's culture from a purely biblical perspective.

BABYLON: THE IDOLATROUS NATION

Babylon the Great—an exotic culture and a people bent on becoming "like God." The innovations of the Babylonians are legend. The Hanging Gardens of Babylon were recognized as one of the all-time great "Seven Wonders of the World." This highly inventive and creative culture was responsible for producing skilled artisans and architects who engineered the impressive Tower of Babel, a fabulous ziggurat intended to be so tall as to reach to heaven so men could ascend to God and speak to Him, on their own terms, whenever they wished. As the Bible indicates, this amazing high-rise project was rooted in rebellion. So what does God do? He brings the whole thing down. He confused the people so bent on invading His domain. And He scrambled the tongues of the workmen, thereby breaking their unity and scattering their forces.

He stopped the Babylonians . . . but only temporarily. A final battle—the battle mentioned in the Book of Revelation—was yet to come, reserved for the End Times, when the forces united by the Antichrist would be pitted against heaven's army in the valley of Armageddon. The same spirit that built Babel will again be the aggressor, because the spirit of Babel was not vanquished with the halting of the Tower project; it simply went underground. When it came up next, it was the force behind the mighty city of Babylon . . . and again, behind the even mightier nation of Babylon, the nation that led the Israelites captive. Trust me—it will rise again . . . in fact, it is already amassing power for its final thrust against mankind.

BABYLON'S ROLE IN HISTORY

God called Babylon to be the wealthiest, most powerful nation ever to exist. In a dream, He revealed this destiny to the great king, Nebuchadnezzar. In Daniel, chapters 1 through 7, the prophet Daniel interpreted the king's dream thus: "You are the head of gold, the highest of it. You are one of the highest human kingdoms."

But Babylon was far more than merely a powerful military empire. It was the birthplace of modern economics. Charging interest on borrowed money originated in Babylon; prior to that, the practice was prohibited. Even after Babylon came up with the concept, some governments prohibited charging interest or what the Bible refers to as *usury* (see Ex. 22:25; Matt. 25:27). *Usury* was created by Babylon but banned by the governments of Israel, Greece, and Rome. In addition, the concept of manipulating supply and demand to control markets and thereby take advantage of the people also originated in Babylon.

Control. They wanted God on their own terms. A thirst for knowledge. An appetite for power. An

The Rise of "Mystery Babylon"

inquisitive nature. An insatiable desire for super-natural intervention. The desire to control and dominate others. These are some of the character-istics of the creative, inventive, highly inquisitive Babylonians who wanted to be in charge and to know the future to such a great degree that they developed the occultic arts as we know them today: palm reading, divination, astrology, temple idolatry, demon sacrifice. All of these forbidden practices sprang from roots in Babylon . . . Mystery Babylon—the birthplace of the occult. Many cults in existence on earth today boast that they can trace their roots back to Babylon. Baal worship, Nimrod's worship of fallen angels, even witchcraft got their starts in Babylon—home of all false reli-gion. A young man once brought me the "holy book" used by a popular cult. As I flipped through its pages, I noticed that the book's editors credited Babylon in the acknowledgments, claiming the cult's genealogy began there.

Mystery Babylon is both a place and a spiritual force on the earth. It was out of Babylon that Abraham was called. The king of Shinar, or Babel, went to Sodom and took Lot and his family cap-tive, and it was against this king that Abraham fought to liberate his relatives. And it was King Nebuchadnezzar that God used to overcome Israel, destroy the temple, and punish the rebel-lious people.

Nebuchadnezzar's dream foretold Babylon's role in history, but also infused him with pride:

> *You looked, O king, and there before you*
> *stood a large statue—an enormous,*

*dazzling statue, awesome in appearance.
The head of the statue was made of pure
gold, its chest and arms of silver, its belly
and thighs of bronze, its legs of iron, its
feet partly of iron and partly of baked
clay. While you were watching, a rock
was cut out, but not by human hands. It
struck the statue on its feet of iron and
clay and smashed them. Then the iron,
the clay, the bronze, the silver, and the
gold were broken to pieces at the same
time and became like chaff on a threshing
floor in the summer. The wind swept them
away without leaving a trace. But the
rock that struck the statue became a huge
mountain and filled the whole earth.
"This was the dream, and now we will
interpret it to the king. You, O king, are
the king of kings. The God of heaven has
given you dominion and power and
might and glory; in your hands He has
placed mankind and the beasts of the
field and the birds of the air. Wherever
they live, he has made you ruler over
them all. You are that head of gold."*

—Daniel 2:31–38

That dream so impressed the king that he "began
to believe his own press," so to speak. God then
judged Nebuchadnezzar, proving that it was God
and not the king who was still in charge. In a powerful open-eyed vision seen by more than just
Nebuchadnezzar, the "moving finger" wrote upon
the palace wall a strange message, again interpreted

The Rise of "Mystery Babylon"

by Daniel: "Thou are weighed in the balances and art found wanting" (Dan. 5:27, KJV). Down came the great king, and down came the once-great Babylonian nation. So much for those "feet of clay."

Babylon may no longer exist, but the spirit of Babylon continues on, operating in a very hidden way behind the scenes. In subtle, hard to define ways, it is setting the stage for the final clash between God's system and the world's system— and the gathering ground is not neutral. The lines are clearly defined. It is the spirit of the world's system, marked by man at the helm versus God's system, where only He is at the helm.

Mystery Babylon is the force behind the evil that has always opposed God and continues to rebel for the right to exist as His equal—something He will never allow. The spirit of Babylon has been around to influence every great nation and every world dominator on the face of the earth since the glory days of Babylon. In every generation, that spirit has encouraged rebellion and self-reliance. It is the spirit of *mammon*—the love of money and things above the love of God or the search for wealth in the absence of God.

THE ULTIMATE END-TIME POWER TRIP

Did you know that God gives man the power to get wealth (Deut. 8:18)? Yet in every generation, the spirit of Babylon has tried to get there first and seduce mankind away from getting wealth God's way and into getting wealth illegally. It's not wealth that God is against; again, it's the lordship issue. The temptation is always there to become sucked in by the world's view of money, power, and pleasure. The spirit of Babylon would like to draw us away from the foundations of the faith. It lures us by tempting us to take wealth and power into our own hands with no thought to God or attention to His spiritual principles regarding finances and their proper stewardship.

The lure of mammon is so subtle yet so strong that it can rarely be detected with the natural eye. It's clothed in darkness and works behind the scenes. Most people can't even see it. Yet at the center of this spiritual influence is a clash between God's system and the world's system, ruled by Mystery Babylon. Only spiritual warfare will equip the Christian to prevail against this demonic force during the last days.

Jesus clearly states that the End Times will be marked with deception (Matt. 24:4–8). What is more potentially deceptive and loaded with danger than the allure of money and things? Unchecked, unfounded love for money and things will inevitably pull us off course in regard to what is of eternal value and what is valuable only in the temporal sense. And if one accepts deception on one level, there is usually an openness to deception in other areas as well. The New Age, for instance, teaches that we are "little gods," able to create our own reality and our own futures—even our own wealth. Do you see what I mean about deception in one area breeding deception in another?

There will be a release of enormous wealth and power during these last days—enough to seduce

The Rise of "Mystery Babylon"

the entire world. Revelation 18:3, states, "For all the nations have drunk the maddening wine of her adulteries. The kings of the earth committed adultery with her, and the merchants of the earth grew rich from her excessive luxuries." This worship of mammon has become a form of spiritual adultery, and it's a hallmark of End-Time deception.

As I have studied the End Times so extensively, I have come to believe that one of the keys to understanding End-Time events is to get a revelation concerning the power of money. It's the battle over finances that will prove one of the most fascinating and most troubling of all the signs, and one of the most fierce End-Time battles for Christians.

The prophet Zechariah saw it coming, and wrote:

> *Then the angel who was speaking to me came forward and said to me, "Look up and see what this is that is appearing." I asked, "What is it?" He replied, "It is a measuring basket." And he added, "This is the iniquity of the people throughout the land." Then the cover of lead was raised, and there in the basket sat a woman! He said, "This is wickedness," and he pushed her back into the basket and pushed the lead cover down over its mouth...." Where are they taking the basket?" I asked the angel who was speaking to me. He replied, "To the country of Babylonia to build a house for it. When it is ready, the basket will be set there in its place."*

—Zechariah 5:5–11

God is saying that one day the spirit of Babylon—this spirit of rebellion against God—shall be unleashed full force during the last days to seduce mankind. It is this spirit through which the antichrist will operate in his global effort to gain control of earth's population. Here's what Revelation has to say about this season just ahead:

After this I saw another angel coming down from heaven. He had great authority, and the earth was illuminated by his splendor. With a mighty voice he shouted: "Fallen! Fallen is babylon the Great! She has become a home for demons and a haunt for every evil spirit, a haunt for every unclean and detestable bird. For all the nations have drunk the maddening wine of her adulteries. The kings of the earth committed adultery with her, and the merchants of the earth grew rich from her excessive luxuries."

Then I heard another voice from heaven say: "Come out of her, my people, so that you will not share in her sins, so that you will not receive any of her plagues; for her sins are piled up to heaven, and God has remembered her crimes. Give back to her as she has given; pay her back double for what she has done. Mix her a double portion from her own cup. Give her as much torture and grief as the glory and luxury she gave herself. In her heart she boasts, 'I sit as a queen; I am not a widow, and I will never mourn.' Therefore, in one day her plagues will overtake her: death, mourning and famine. She will be consumed by fire, for mighty is the Lord God who judges her.

"When the kings of the earth who committed adultery with her and shared her luxury see the smoke of her burning, they will weep and mourn over her. Terrified at her torment, they will stand far off and cry: 'Woe! Woe, O great city, O Babylon, city of power! In one hour your doom has come!'... They will throw dust on their heads, and with weeping and mourning cry out: 'Woe! Woe, O great city, where all who had ships on the sea became rich through her wealth! In one hour she has been brought to ruin! Rejoice over her, O heaven! Rejoice, saints and apostles and prophets! God has judged her for the way she treated you.'"

—Revelation 18:1–10, 19–20

Contained in this passage of text is the prophetic picture of the final rise—and fall—of Mystery Babylon. Here, we receive the promise of the eventual collapse of this world economic system built by man, not God. But it's not just about money. It's about the collapse of civilization itself, because it turned to go its own way and forgot God entirely.

◆ ◆ ◆

MONEY MAKES THE WORLD GO 'ROUND

Money. Some think it's gauche to talk money in public. To others, it's a symbol of power. Money drives—has always driven—the world's economy. It has the potential to deceive, or it can be used for God's glory. It can distract, derail, destroy. Or it can be used correctly to further the kingdom of God. To understand the power of money is to understand the root motives of the hearts of men. Financial needs, problems, and desires explain many of the strange decisions that we see unfolding around us in these End Times. In fact, it is money—not war, not famine, not pestilence—that will drive most major End-Time events. For End-Time economics is the tool by which the Antichrist will "deceive many." The great events of biblical prophecy, written many hundreds of years ago, are intricately woven on the golden threads of mammon.

Manipulation of End-Time supply and demand will ultimately give rise to a resurrected Roman Empire, from which will spring a false "world church" and an unbelievably powerful "one world" political system presided over by the Antichrist.

Then, according to Revelation, chapter 13, the beast will come with power. There will be a mark associated with his coming—a mark all people must take upon themselves in order to function in the forum of his domain. That mark will provide access to the world's financial system; without it, people will be prohibited from buying, selling, trading—even from purchasing the basic necessities of life. The number, according to the Bible, is 666 (Rev. 13:18).

The Rise of "Mystery Babylon"

The Bible states that the mark will be permanently affixed to one's forehead or arm. Seemed pretty far-fetched until recently, when micro-technology exploded onto the scene with the advent of the space program. In NASA's ongoing efforts to lighten the payloads into space, computer components became smaller and smaller, with the technological advances spilling over into the fields of medicine and even household gadgets. Now there is the internet and on-line banking, international finance networks capable of electronically transferring large sums of money at the click of a button. And credit card technology promises to "read" human thumbprints—among other personalized theft-proof devices—all in a card small enough to fit into one's palm. These are no longer the idle ramblings of wild-eyed prophets who lived centuries ago; the technology is here, and it's real.

Dogs and other small animals are already recipients of this cutting-edge technology. An injection device can insert microchips for identification purposes beneath the skin of animals that go everywhere with them. It's no secret that the same technology, if applied to humans, would enable one to carry one's financial history and current status literally "on them" at all times. We're there—and it's a matter of time before the pressure will go on to make everyone conform to this new techno-craze.

It will sound so smooth and so rational—even good for us. We'll be told it's so we can keep pace with the world's exploding technology and the global economy. We'll be told, "Take it, or you won't be able to participate in commerce." What they won't tell you at first is that if you don't take it, you will die. Nor will they tell you that if you do take it, you will be denying God and His power. If you take it, you deny God; if you don't take it, you'll die. That's the choice.

The big question is how anyone would take upon themselves the mark of the beast, knowing its danger?

Why, indeed? Need and desire have always done strange things to people.

A SMOOTH-TALKING DUDE

You may say the Antichrist will be the consummate "smooth-talking dude." Here he is from out of nowhere promising an end to the problems that even now are escalating worldwide. He will promise to solve all these enormous social, political, and economic problems—and for three-and-a-half years, he will seem to be just what the world has needed. Consider how we'd appreciate such a man if he could indeed reduce America's national debt by five hundred million dollars a year and at the same time remove the illegal drug traffic and stop 80 percent of all crime. What a guy!

But that's not all—it's just the warm-up act. He promises an answer to the problem of missing children, and due to his intervention in business and employment, he even legislates a way to save you six hours of your time a week—six hours with which you can play and pursue more leisure activities. He promises to instill confidence and restores our rightful position of undisputed leader once more on the landscape of world politics.

He brings nothing but stability and breeds nothing but confidence.

Would you vote for such a man?

Believe me, he's coming, and he'll be elected—especially if he presents himself as a friend of God and Israel. Especially if he seems religious.

"So what?" you may say.

But if you ask, "What will it cost?" I'll tell you: In fact, I'm glad you asked. It will cost nothing at all. It's free. All this problem-solving comes absolutely, 100 percent free of charge. No higher taxes. In fact, I believe we'll even have lower taxes. Impossible?

Not if all this will be done within the framework of a cashless society—and remember, we're edging closer toward such a cashless society every second. What comes with it is a totally unified world economic system in which individual countries lose both their unique financial complexion and their control over their portion of the global financial picture.

Here's what *USA Today* had to say about such a society at the beginning of the nineties:

> *Imagine a "cashless society" where you can get groceries and gas, dine on fast food, and make a phone call—all without a dime in your pocket. Robert Bamone, president of Diebold, Inc., an automated teller machine manufacturer, forecast such a future; "You will soon be able to do anything that you do today, without*

*cash or credit cards that can be stolen,
through skin implants or invisible tatoos.*"

Fortune magazine says the cashless system will save billions a year in needless paperwork and time. Banks say it will save millions of man-hours and stop theft because theft isn't as easy if there's no cash to steal. Cash, after all, is the most stolen of all commodities. Market analysts say the cashless way will inevitably destroy the illegal drug trade, because almost all drug transactions leave a clear paper trail. Transactions involving huge sums of money could be easily monitored, with the kingpins soon targeted and sent to jail.

An article in *Time* magazine states: "Your report on drug smugglers converting drug-tinged money into clean assets shows that our government's oversupply of U.S. currency is a prime case of the growth of the cocaine trade. The way to catch them is through a surprise big-cash recall. Kiss crime good-bye."

Some Christians even appear to support the cashless system. Author William G. Ridgeway writes: "Cash is the criminal's vital accomplice. . . . Cash, in short, is the root of a heck of a lot of the world's evils, and we must outlaw it. On a foldable card the size of a dollar bill, we will imprint an astonishing amount of information. Bank balances, credit limits, criminal records, medical records, passport, driver's license, welfare eligibility, and other data including your thumbprint making theft worthless to a thief. The benefit? The sale of illegal drugs would stop, the spread of AIDS would be curtailed as drug use fades away.

The Rise of "Mystery Babylon"

The cost of government would go down. So would the cost of private business. The end of tax evasion—payment in cash to avoid sales tax and income tax—would add hundreds of billions of dollars to the government's coffers."

Sounds almost too good to be true, doesn't it? I mean, all we would have to do is give up a little freedom and a little privacy—and we'd get so much back . . . wouldn't we? Wouldn't it all be worth it to have no more missing children, no more credit-card theft, no more bank robberies, no more illegal drug traffic, and a reduction in the AIDS epidemic? Now, wouldn't all that be worth a microchip injection telling everything about us known to man? How could any of us resist such an offer?

After all, the world's a bad place and getting worse even as you read this. *USA Today* reports, "Ever-rising lawlessness to contend with will cause the public to demand more and more repressive measures for safety and prosperity's sake. People will give them up when it hits their standard of living."

Would you?

How much freedom are you willing to give up for a little more peace of mind, a lot less crime, and a higher standard of living that would surely be the result?

No More Fiction

Fiction? Not anymore. Fact. In today's economy,

these are present-day realities. Cashless transactions. National economies linked by electronic network to enable fast transfer of money without anyone ever seeing a dollar bill change hands. America's third largest grocery store chain is leading the way in terms of the cashless method by developing a card that will enable you to buy groceries without check, cash, or credit card. You can now buy groceries and other goods over the internet. Some of America's colleges have been totally cashless for several years. The world economy is not fiction; it's here.

I'm not saying don't participate in global economics, and I'm not saying don't be entrepreneurial. I'm not saying don't make money, and I'm not saying don't get wealth. What I am saying is know the Word of God, and heed the warnings it contains regarding End-Time economics. I am also saying that you must make your mind up now regarding certain issues where compromise is concerned, for there will come a moment when you must choose God's way . . . or the way of Mystery Babylon. One of these days, you're going to have to choose. . . .

"It's optional," you may say.

Sorry. That's where you're wrong. Taking the mark will be neither optional to the world's system, nor optional to God's. If you take it, you go against God. If you don't—well, you know what the Bible says will happen if you don't take the mark.

"Protesting too loudly isn't going to help either, because the disturbance you kick up is going to end up in one of your files," says Terry Galanoy, the former director of communications for Visa International. "And on that 'come and get it' day when we're totally dependent upon our card—or whatever survival device might replace it—you will be left all alone without one." That commercial for a popular credit card that boasts, "Don't leave home without it," may be optional today; tomorrow it won't be.

What is even more amazing about these developments in the world's economy is that God predicted the day in which you and I live, and two thousand years ago gave us prophetic indicators by which we would know the times. I remember sitting and listening to sermons preached twenty years ago about that computer in Belgium called "the beast." Even though it sounded pretty interesting, I thought, *No way! That will never be! Forget it—that computer in Belgium is not the beast the Bible speaks of. No way!* Well, the computer that once filled an entire room in Belgium is now pocket-sized and can fit in the palm of my hand. And it's getting smaller every day. I'm not as skeptical as I was twenty years ago.

Listen to the Word of God:

> *He [the Antichrist] was given power to give breath to the image of the first beast, so that it could speak and cause all who refused to worship the image to be killed. He also forced everyone, small and great, rich and poor, free and slave, to receive a mark on his right hand or on his forehead, so that no one could buy or sell unless he had the mark, which is the*

name of the beast or the number of his name. This calls for wisdom. If anyone has insight, let him calculate the number of the beast, for it is man's number. His number is 666.

—Revelation 13:15–18

I'm not saying don't have credit cards. Remember, I'm no fanatic. But let's say Visa and MasterCard and American Express are just the beginning. Where do you draw the line? Just how far will you go before you are no longer willing to be a player in the world's economic system?

There is a method to all this madness; the world's economy is not shaping up the way it is simply because it's simpler to carry no cash. The reason is that such a society was prophesied two thousand years ago as part of the plan of the Antichrist to overtake the world and gain control of mankind. His purpose is not to bless and save us time and money but to deceive and ultimately destroy. And he will lead the way to destruction via Mystery Babylon.

So what's the danger in a little mammon now and then? The danger is this: God and mammon are in direct opposition. It's always been so. It will always be so. Let me elaborate: God is not against money and neither am I. God is not against wealth and things; He made them! Money in and of itself, as I have already stated, is neither good nor evil. But the focus has to be on God in order for money to be held in the proper perspective. When money, not God, gets control of us, there is a word for it—and that word is *mammon. Mammon* involves more than just money; it is money that is alive. Mammon is that powerful force of wealth gotten without God's control or sanction or blessing.

Mammon seeks wealth independent of God, emphasizes self-rule, and accepts no guilt, responsibility, or obligation. Fun, freedom, and the pursuit of pleasure—that's what it's all about when the spirit of mammon gets a foothold. "Don't tell me how to run it; I just want to have a good time with no guilt and none of this religious stuff!" This is the slippery downhill slope, and it will suck mankind right along with its empty promises of security without sacrifice, pleasure without pleasing God.

Materialism, after all, is nothing new; it's been around forever. *Webster's* defines it as nothing more than "a preoccupation with, or the tendency to seek after or stress material things rather than spiritual things as defining success." The *Thorndike and Barnhart Junior Dictionary* defines a materialist as "a person who cares too much for the things of this world and neglects spiritual needs and purposes." So mammon—materialism—is not about possessions or wealth, but about their power over us. It's about the surrender to pleasure versus the surrender to God. A good example of this misplaced emphasis is the story of the rich farmer in Luke, chapter 12. Here was a man who was rich in terms of material goods but who was not rich toward God and his fellowman.

First Timothy 6:9–10 states, "People who want to get rich fall into temptation and a trap and into many foolish and harmful desires that plunge men into ruin and destruction. For the love of money is the root of all kinds of evil. Some people, eager for money, have wandered from the faith and pierced themselves with many griefs."

Materialism, however, is not a battle based on a person's economic status. We all fight it at one time or another. The issue is a "heart issue,"not a "social issue." It involves everyone, rich or poor. The world is always pulling at us, trying to draw us away with the latest get-rich-quick scheme, and the temptation is ever before us to put money before God. A millionaire can be blessed of God and free from the power and pull of money. A poor man can be covered up under a load of materialism, ruled by the spirit of mammon, and still be on food stamps and living from handout to handout. Again, it is not just the wealthy who are given to greed, envy, bitterness, and materialism. As Howard Hendricks observed, "Materialism has nothing to do with the amount. It has everything to do with the attitude. What owns you?"

SO WHAT CAN WE DO ABOUT IT?

Is there no hope in fighting against the force of Mystery Babylon? Of course there's hope. Jesus is our hope, and His prophetic word to us centuries ago provides both a warning and a way out.

There is a way of escape and a means by which we can live in God's blessing under true prosperity without being dragged down by the world's godless system. Here is some practical help for living free of the entanglements of Mystery Babylon during the End Time.

The Rise of "Mystery Babylon"

• *BE HONEST.*

Open your heart to God and be honest enough to admit that the pull of mammon is there all around you. Money, after all, is a main cause of divorce and depression, and the Bible speaks of it more often than any other single subject. So deal with it, up front, openly and honestly, in prayer. Tell God about it, and listen as the Holy Spirit begins to adjust your attitudes regarding money and the system of the world. So be honest enough to open your heart to God and let Him steer you around the hidden obstacles in your path.

• *REMEMBER YOU ARE NOT ALONE IN THIS BATTLE; IT'S A UNIVERSAL ONE.*

God is saying, "Relax! I know you're battling in this area of finances. That's why I'm talking to you about it right now!" The key to winning is not in the denial but in the discussion. Remember, this is a worldwide spiritual attack—not a specific targeted attack against just you. Everyone of us faces financial pressures of economic needs and desires in our daily lives. None of us is free of these pressures. God understands. Temptation is not a sin, but we must be honest enough to admit temptation exists and seek God's help in delivering us from the temptations.

• *REFUSE TO BE ENSLAVED BY MYSTERY BABYLON.*

Be free! By that, I mean avoid the financial slavery that comes with indebtedness. God's command is, "Get out!" His simple plan of deliverance can be found in Revelation 18:4, which states: "Then I heard another voice from heaven say: 'Come out of her, my people, so that you will not share in her sins, so that you will not receive any of her plagues.'" It's time to get out! You cannot escape the influence of the spirit of the age— mammon—but you can be free of its power. You can't turn back the clock, but you can simplify your financial picture to jettison the debt load that's weighing you down. The great danger of Babylon is not in its wealth but in the bondage that comes with its debt. As H. W. F. Saggs observed in his book, *The Greatness That Was Babylon,* "The economic development of judicious loans were able to oppress the poor, the wealthy man making the poor man a loan and then foreclosing at an inconvenient time, taking in an animal or other goods of the debtor far exceeding the amount of the loan . . . ." This system of usury was invented in Babylon, and it oppresses us still. It's a system of carefully applied and increased pressure, intimidation, greed, and loss. Debt—get out of it, and stay out!

- **LIVE SIMPLY.**

By that, I mean finding happiness not in things but in the eternal, big-picture issues—people, life, love, serving God and others.

- **SEPARATE YOUR NEEDS FROM YOUR DESIRES.**

That one's pretty easy to identify and pretty hard to do, especially if you have already developed the habit of yielding to your desires. You're going to have to tighten up in a few areas, and you're probably going to have to seek God's help in doing it. So again, pray; ask God to help you forego the short-term gain for the long-range vision. Then allow Christ to bless you in His way, and in His time. The Bible says that when He blesses, He "adds no sorrow with it" (Prov. 10:22, NKJV).

• PRACTICE DEFERRED GRATIFICATION.

Want it? You can have it—but save for it, don't borrow so you can have it right now. Do you see what I mean? Do it God's way, and you'll be stronger as a result. Also, don't borrow for perishable things. Don't go into debt for food, clothing, and other short-term items that will be used up or worn out long before the debt connected to them has been settled. The spirit of Babylon is the spirit of oppressive debt. Watch out!

• BE OBEDIENT!

Train your heart to be sensitive to the Holy Spirit's direction, and follow His leadership. Obey His still, small voice. Learn to be submissive to the Holy Spirit now, because it will only become harder as we move further into the End-Time season. Remember that often the Holy Spirit's direction makes no sense and, more often than that, goes against our wants and our desires. But He knows best, and His will for us is good. Sometimes His direction is more about trusting Him than about obedience. That's why, for no apparent reason, He'll tell us, No! when we're about to do something or make some financial decision that appears to be no big deal. It looks like a great deal, so it must be one. Right? Not necessarily. The Holy Spirit knows right where all those hidden snares are located, so when you go against His leading, you regret it. Every day of my life the Holy Spirit tells me no. In fact, He tells me no more often than He tells me yes. I don't like hearing no. The times I've gone against it, I've regretted doing so. It's as if I'm telling God, "I want it. I can afford it. I can do it! It's my money!" and He's responding back, "You want it? You can do it. Just remember I told you so!" He always seems to have the last word!

- ***DO NOT HARDEN YOUR HEART.***

Keep yourself open to the will of God and His voice by listening to Him and obeying His direction. Repent when you mess up, and you'll find your heart remains tender toward the Lord. God calls us to keep a tender heart and to guard against becoming resistant or rebellious to His will. "Do not harden your hearts as you did in the rebellion, during the time of testing in the desert, where your fathers tested and tried me and for forty years saw what I did. That is why I was angry with that generation, and I said, 'Their hearts are always going astray, and they have not known my ways.' So I declared an oath in my anger, 'They shall never enter my rest.' See to it, brothers, that none of you has a sinful, unbelieving heart that turns away from the living God" (Heb. 3:8–12).

The Rise of "Mystery Babylon"

An old Indian proverb goes like this: "Disobeying the voice of God is like a knife in our heart. It hurts the first time. Every time we disobey God, the knife turns and hurts more . . . until the day comes when it does not hurt any longer because the knife has made a hole in our heart. No more pain. No more voice of God." Just as a parent warns a child who's standing in the path of an oncoming car, so the Holy Spirit sees what's coming in the future and warns us. We must learn to obey now so we will be prepared for what is coming.

• *BE GENEROUS.*

The ultimate test of whether or not we're winning the war against mammon is generosity. It's the test of giving. If we are able to give generously to God and others, we're winning. We may think that because we've worked so hard, we should be entitled to keep 100 percent of the proceeds, but that's not what God says. His economy operates a little differently. If we give, He gives. If we cannot give, we're in bondage, and this bondage ultimately leads to poverty, lack, and wrong decisions in the financial realm. God is calling His people to generosity and faithful giving. How will we ever trust Him in the tough times when we haven't learned how to give today? Read what Malachi 3:10–14 says about giving, and then apply those principles. It states that if we give to God, He will open up heaven's storehouses and give back to us; if we don't, we're cursed.

Proverbs 3:9–10, states: "Honor the Lord with

your wealth, with the firstfruits of all your crops; then your barns will be filled to overflowing, and your vats will brim over with new wine." There are two kingdoms with two sets of resources. There is God's kingdom, presided over by Jesus Christ, and there is man's kingdom, ruled by the spirit of Babylon. Which will it be? God's way is one of faith, giving, sacrifice, freedom, generosity, success, and blessing. Man's way is bondage, greed, selfishness, storing up, and success without God's blessing. Trust God! Learn to give, because money and the fear of losing it can control you and suck all the joy right out of you. Freedom in the financial realm depends on generosity— expectant, joyful giving that glorifies the God of miracles.

• *Put Christ at the top of your priorities list.*

Choose by faith to pursue His great plan and purpose for your life. It's not wrong to have dreams and desires and goals other than those pertaining to the kingdom. But it's wrong and even dangerous to allow those desires and goals to occupy a higher position than Jesus Christ on your list of priorities. Matthew 6:31–33, states, "Do not worry, saying, 'What shall we eat?' or 'What shall we drink?' or 'What shall we wear?' For the pagans run after all these things, and your heavenly Father knows that you need them. But seek first his kingdom and his righteousness, and all these things will be given to you as well."

The Rise of "Mystery Babylon"

- *DETERMINE TO BE A WINNER IN THE LAST DAYS.*

There is success . . . and then there is success *God's way*. Determine to go God's way. Be honest! Be courageous! Be generous! Be sensitive to the voice of the Holy Spirit! Keep your focus on the Lord! And you will win the battle against the spirit of the world and its economic system.

There you have it—God's way out of Babylon. For the end is near . . . but not yet. So don't be afraid. Be bold. Go God's way, and you'll be blessed.

4

THE ONE-WORLD RELIGION

U *nity was a very big deal to Babylon of old.* It's still a very big deal. The spirit of Babylon relies on unity and the power amassed by unity, in order to operate in such an oppressive, forceful way against mankind. We just examined in chapter three what a unified world economic system will mean to earth's population. In this chapter, we'll take a look at the coming one-world religious movement. This powerful religious movement may come in the name of love and peace and brotherhood, but believe me—at its roots are corruption and deception— anything but love and peace and brotherhood.

The object is to oppress us and to pull us off course with God, just as it has always been the object throughout history.

It's interesting to note that for every move of God throughout history there has been a corresponding counterfeit attempt to deceive mankind and draw people away from a real move of God. The most high God prophesied to Adam and Eve in the garden, just after the Fall, that He would send a Redeemer—the seed of a woman—to bruise the head of the serpent, Satan (Gen. 3:15). So as far back as the glory days of Babylon, Satan was already scheming to send in a cheap counterfeit of the Son of God—a tawdry imitation of the real thing—the Redeemer of fallen man.

Revealed on ancient stone tablets excavated from ancient Babylon, King Nimrod, Satan's cheesy counterfeit of Jesus Christ, takes an evil wife (Gen. 10). First to rebel against God, Nimrod marries Semiramis, who prides herself in having lain with Lucifer, the fallen angel who became known as Satan (Gen. 10:8). Thus arises the foundation of a powerful false religion with striking similarities to Christianity:

1. Nimrod's queen gives birth to a son—the son of Lucifer—who saves the empire.

2. Queen Semiramis becomes known throughout the land as the queen of heaven, and worship of mother and child becomes standard practice.

3. In every generation thereafter, and in

every culture, this mother/son worship can be found; ancient statues show Semiramis as queen of heaven, and her son, Tammuz, as savior of her empire—the earth below.

4. Tammuz dies, then—empowered by his father, Lucifer—is raised from the dead to conquer and save the world.

Sounds a lot like Christianity, doesn't it? But remember, all this was recorded on stone in Babylon, two thousand years before the birth of Christ. Babylon by then had already aligned itself with the powers of darkness, and Satan's master plan to deceive mankind was already well under way.

As far back as two thousand years before the birth of Christ, that plan to bring forth this counterfeit religious system, diametrically opposed to Christianity, was already in gear. A leader had already been prepared. Then his name was Tammuz. When he next appears, he will be known as the Antichrist.

FROM BABYLON: THE BEAST WHO DIES AND LIVES AGAIN

Revelation 13:12–23, states: "He exercised all the authority of the first beast on his behalf, and made the earth and its inhabitants worship the first beast, whose fatal wound had been healed. And he performed great and miraculous signs, even causing fire to come down from heaven to earth in full view of man." From this text, we see the Antichrist will appear to die then be raised from the dead in order to fulfill the ancient Babylonian prophecy of Tammuz's death and resurrection.

What's wrong with this picture? You'd have to be pretty discerning in order the separate the real from the fake when this Tammuz guy bursts upon the scene once more. Smooth, charming, filled with power, and able to schmooze, this natural-born leader will look like, sound like, lead like the guy God sent to do the job on earth. What's more, he'll seem very religious and upright—a guy with all the right answers. But remember, he is Tammuz—born out of Babylon where temple prostitution and the occultic arts originated, the place where astrology, mediums, and divination were born, not to mention contact with the dead and sacrifice of animals and humans to a whole series of demon gods. That is the religion that will be backing up this guy who'll look and sound so good.

This is the stuff of the Antichrist—the stuff that will mark the End Times and make it more necessary now than ever to have "eyes to see" and "ears to hear" (see Ezek. 12:2). Because God will judge this false religion, those who participate in it will come under severe judgment at the White Throne judgment of God.

Whether they know it or not, God's people have had many encounters with this spirit of Tammuz at various times throughout history. Ezekiel writes that God would judge the people because they mixed ceremonies in worship of

The One-World Religion

Tammuz with the worship of Jehovah (Ezek. 8:14–18). He protests against the people of God "weeping for Tammuz" in God's own temple. The prophet Jeremiah actually pronounces a curse on the people of God for such mixture of worship. In Jeremiah 7:18–20, the prophet writes that those who make cakes for the queen of heaven and mix these practices in with the feasts of Jehovah will be cursed. That's right—the priests were doing double-duty, offering up harmless little cakes to demonic spirits in Solomon's Temple while they attempted to offer up acceptable worship to God. Jeremiah said, "Stop it!"

Throughout the Bible, there are many references to Baal worship, Israel's great sin, rooted in the demon-worship of Babylon. God ordered His leaders to go throughout the land and "tear down the high places"—destroy the sites where the baals were worshiped by the people of God. Again and again God raised up leaders who made war against the priests of baal, going through the land to tear down the high places . . . but some always managed to remain. At no time were the forbidden practices entirely removed from the land of Israel—just as at no time since the beginning of this demonic plot on earth has there been an absence of such activity regarding this false religious system.

Today it's packaged with the label of "peace and love" and called various things—the New Age, Universalism, the One-World movement. Just as Christians are called to live in brotherhood and unity, esteeming each other more highly than themselves, and just as the Jews are marked by their deeply rooted ability to live together in community, so also has this one-world religious movement risen to counterfeit the same traits. But laced with these seemingly harmless religious practices are the seeds and roots of Babylonian occultism. Otherwise, why would a New Ager cling so closely to their favorite crystals or wed pagan-istic meditation and candle-burning with a belief in reincarnation and past lives, then cap the whole thing off with terms like "Christ consciousness"?

We must have eyes to see and ears to hear these subtle and not-so-subtle differences that separate the real from the counterfeit in this hour. Revelation 17 clearly details the rise and fall of just such a counterfeit religious system on earth shortly before the return of Christ.

THE REAL VS. THE FAKE

Now let me explain to you how this thing works so you'll get a picture of these events unfolding: What we have here is an actual type of the false church's aligning itself with the false christ. Again, we see the image of a woman. As Christ will come for His bride, so the Antichrist will come for his bride—the harlot-woman and her false religious system mentioned in Revelation 17:1: "Come, I will show you the punishment of the great prosti-tute, who sits on many waters."

What is a harlot (prostitute) but one who sells herself for money? She is unfaithful, not to be trusted, mercenary, and deceptive. She is not just immoral; she is out to seduce . . . to take people away from Christ. She seduces and is also seduced.

In contrast, there is the pure bride of Christ, without spot or wrinkle, kept for Him, faithful and prepared for His glory and honor. Christ is coming back for a purified people. He is purifying His people and making them ready for His glorious return. That purifying, I believe, is responsible for a lot of the shaking and sifting going on today throughout the body of Christ. As the counterfeit seduces and, in turn, is seduced, so the bride of Christ becomes purer and purer, more and more glorious until she shines forth with the glory of God Himself. Remember that word *purity,* because standing in stark contrast to it will be the deceptive, dark practices of the false one-world church.

Revelation 17:4 states that this harlot church is both rich and powerful—another root we can trace back to Babylon. "And the woman was arrayed in purple and scarlet color, and decked with gold and precious stones and pearls, having a golden cup in her hand full of abominations and filthiness of her fornication" (v. 4, KJV). She uses money and power to persecute true believers, because she hates the true move of God—the church. Revelation 17:6 reveals that she actually becomes drunk on the blood of the saints. She appears to have the edge, to be winning, all-powerful, all-successful in her efforts to deceive the innocent and persecute the discerning. But wait—there's another side to this aspect of seducing and being seduced. The harlot becomes enamored with herself—drunk on her own power. This ultimately leads to her own destruction, because she becomes distracted by all that power. In other words, she is not alert.

Christians, on the other hand, are called to alert in this hour. We are mandated to watch and know the seasons of the End Times. That's why Jesus dropped the prophecy bomb in Matthew, chapter 24: He wanted to warn His people and prepare them to win against the harlot and the beast. Can you see the way the two will cooperate in the last days to overcome and overpower all mankind?

There is virtually no way, in fact, for you to look at the two entities—the one-world economic/government system and the one-world religion—because they are so wedded and entwined with one another that they are indistinguishable separately. Even with all that power shared between them, the Bible clearly states that in the end, we win: "The beast and the ten horns you saw will hate the prostitute. They will bring her to ruin and leave her naked; they will eat her flesh and burn her with fire" (Rev. 17:16).

"Okay," you may say, "there have always been one-world movements—both in government and in religion. How is this one different from all the others?" The difference is that today you are watching the alignment of anti-Christian forces against Christians who are seen globally as the enemy. For the first time in history, religions who have nothing in common other than the fact that they are not Christian, are linking up against Christianity to give one unified message: "You're excluded!" Regardless of their opposite perspectives and radically different goals, they have one very large persuasion in common: Christianity is the foe. Christians have been hedged out of this global religious move, and Christians have been lumped together and branded as rigid, egotistical, hypocritical, Bible-thumping radicals.

At a recent gathering of world religious leaders in San Francisco, California, sixty-five hundred representatives of various religious groups met to discuss this one-world religious movement. Curiously absent were the evangelicals. As an article in the *Times* stated in response to the question of why there were no evangelicals present, "These people are uncooperative. They are hard-lined. They don't want to dialogue; and therefore, we decided to work around them." That about says it all, doesn't it?

Old News . . . and New News

Crystals, chants, channeling, holistic healers, and hatha yoga, mantras and meditation—New Age power cults and psychic networks, reincarnation as the ultimate recognition of human potential in the absence of God—these dogmas have become so much a part of the global landscape that we don't even pay attention to them anymore. It's all old news. But what's new news is this: the New Age has moved from a recognizable movement into the classrooms and boardrooms, its secular worldview infecting everything from curricula materials to corporate training instruments so that whether we want to acknowledge it or not, we are being slowly, subtly injected with New Age influences even if we're not paying attention to what's going on. Let me share some quotes with you:

I see images of a new heaven and a new earth. This world will be saved. The planet will be healed and harmonized. We can let the kingdom come . . . which means this world can be transformed into heaven right now! This is not fantasy. This is not scientific or religious fiction. This is the main event of our lives, our future. We have high expectations, we are intoxicated with the possibility.

—John Randolph Price
Organizer of World Peace Day

Nothing will be accomplished by ourselves, but together there is nothing we cannot do. We are the architects of our own destiny because we have the power of thought and the power of choice. We are the only ones who will save this earth.

—Dennis Weaver
star of television's *McCloud*

The future is not for the faint-hearted, it is even more certainly not for the cowardly. . . . Those who insist that theirs is the only correct government or economic system deserve the same contempt as those who insist that they have the only true God.

—Gene Roddenberry
creator of *Star Trek*

The One-World Religion

Sounds good, doesn't it—I mean, all this tolerance for one another? What's wrong with a little compromise? I mean, there's nothing wrong with Jesus; we like Jesus. Muslims like Jesus; New Age people like Jesus . . . in fact, they want to *become* Him and believe they will if they chant hard enough and get good enough and live enough lifetimes. Who minds Jesus being around? Just don't proclaim that He is "the way, the truth, and the life"! If we do that, we're claiming there is just one way. And in the current one-world movement, there are many ways proposed to heaven, not just one. Sounds a bit like Babel to me.

The Bible clearly states that there is one God, one Savior, one Lord, and one Way. Jesus is the Way. *The only Way.*

Why is that so threatening to the governments and religious systems of the world? Why, indeed? Because in that one name, there is enough power to defeat all counterfeits—even the harlot and the beast.

THE LINES ARE BEING DRAWN

The world is quickly dividing into two camps— Christians, and everyone else. In the Christian camp are those who look to Christ alone as their Lord, their savior, their answer, and the way to heaven. In the other camp are those who look to other gods, their own strength, outward influences such as astrology and divination and channeling, and even to human wisdom and achievement as the answer.

This clash between the two religious camps is edging closer. In my home state of North Carolina, the pledge of allegiance to the United States has been outlawed. Why? Because those in state government believe it infringes on the civil rights of some of its citizens and teaches children allegiance to just one state instead of allegiance to the "global village." Give me a break! But that's one of the waves we're riding, according to the nation's number-one best-seller, *Megatrends 2000:* "Around the New Millennium 2000 there will come a unifying of religions around the world with economics and politics to bring peace to the world."

New Age author Ruth Montgomery, who began her career as a White House journalist and now writes books on occult topics, is said to have "channeled" a group to the future. There, they found that the earth had shifted on its axis around the year 2000, bringing about a period of peace that would last a thousand years. Where have we heard all this before? Montgomery writes: "An antichrist who has already been born will be the powerful world leader."

According to the magazine, *The Futurist,* a group called URO—United Religions Organized—is "quickly gathering strength to unite religion, economics, and politics into a world peace power. We are just looking for our leader."

That leader will probably be both political and religious in nature—a smooth politician with global vision and religious-sounding rhetoric. The foundation from which such a man springs has already been laid. Hear what former Senator Barry Goldwater has to say on the subject of the

The One-World Religion

Trilateral Commission: "Whereas the Council of Foreign Relations is distinctively national in membership, the Trilateral Commission is international. Representation is allocated equally to Western Europe, Japan, and the United States. It is intended to be the world consolidator by seizing control of the government of the United States. The Trilateral Commission represents a skillful, coordinated effort to seize control and consolidate the force and centers of power, politically, monetary, intellectual, and religious. As managers and creators of this system, they will control the future." This is from a leading national politician and a man who once ran for the U.S. presidency.

You may think this is the bad news; it's not. There have always been nutcakes around with a thirst for power and a plan to get it. The bad news is that Christians appear to be buying into this nonsense. I can understand those who don't know Christ wandering into this maze of political and religious intrigue in their bid for personal power, but Christians? I expect those who have been raised in Bible-believing churches to know better.

What is alarming to me is that those who call themselves "Christians" are beginning to align themselves with this "world religious freedom" movement. Some are beginning to embrace and espouse New Age ideas, and these ideas are coming out in their pulpits, in their prayers, and in the pages of the books they write. An article in the December 1994 issue of *Psychology Today* stated that a "new spiritual awakening" is occurring amid an absence of organized methods. "Catholics may practice Buddhist meditating, Jews may be a member of a Moslem Sufi group."

It leads me to wonder about the foundations of what such people claim to believe. Were the foundations ever laid in? For instance, three fourths of adults who say they're Christians also believe that they will go to heaven on the basis of their own merit. Three fourths of all adult Christians actually believe they're going to heaven because they've been good and done good works for God.

In addition, a majority of Christians believe there's more than just one way to heaven, and that Christianity is only one of them. This concept is being taught in some of our leading seminaries, by the way. No wonder Christians are so confused about what they believe. But this confusion is not limited to adults; teens are also wondering what to believe. A survey of thirty-seven hundred teenagers conducted by Josh McDowell revealed that "57 percent of young people from families actively involved in their church say there is no objective standard of truth."

A majority of Christians don't believe that God operates in the realm of the supernatural, or that He performs miracles today. They state that they no longer expect God to become actively involved in their lives, or to hear their prayers, or to respond back with direction and counsel. They no longer believe He speaks to their hearts. They perceive Him as some unseen force of wisdom and esoteric guidance—just a "thing." Another author observed that not only are we living in a post-Christian culture but that a majority of those who call themselves Christians "are really atheists." Can you

The One-World Religion

believe it? I can believe it. In fact, it fits right in with the one-world movement as headed up by the Antichrist, because between now and the moment that he is revealed, the antichrist spirit is already at work laying the foundation for his false world platform.

But the hatred of these one-world adherents against Christians has heated up in the last few decades, and the fires of hatred will burn even brighter between now and the return of Christ. According to *Christianity Today,* more Christians have been martyred for Christ in this decade than at any other time in history. (For a survey of this anti-Christian activity around the world, see *Their Blood Cries Out* by Paul Marshall with Lela Gilbert.) People are getting killed for the cause of Christ, and it's so ignored in the secular press that people in Lubbock, Texas, or Orlando, Florida, or San Francisco, or New York City never even hear about it. But when it starts happening in Lubbock and Orlando and San Francisco and New York, what then?

Why is there so much animosity building against Christians, and why do we even need to become aware of it? Why don't we fit into the world's system, and why don't the architects of the one-world religion include us in their ranks?

The answer is simple: we're in battle. (see Ephesians 6:12–18.)

The Bible says the Christian is involved in daily spiritual warfare, whether or not they even realize it, and that we have been given a series of weapons with which to fight the battle for the church—and win.

5

THE BATTLE FOR THE CHURCH

he battle for the church is going to heat up: You can count on that. I believe God is getting His people ready to engage in spiritual warfare of greater intensity and at deeper levels than we have ever experienced on earth. He's calling us to sharpen our swords, polish our weapons, get ready, and stay on the alert so that when the time comes, we'll be armed and dangerous against the enemy.

In my opinion, most people miss one important point when they consider the End Times and the events leading up to the glorious return of Christ—the fact that for every scripture verse about the Tribulation, the Antichrist, the rapture, or the beast, there are *five* verses about the great spiritual battle that will face God's people in the End Times. This is the area where God focuses most of His instruction regarding the last days. This great spiritual battle is not well-known because it's rarely being taught. The enemy's attacks against Christians in the End Times are both silent and subtle, and so we just don't talk about them, thinking that if we ignore them the attacks may go away. They won't go away; they're going to increase. And we'd better pay attention, because—like it or not—we're going to be involved in this last great battle between the people of God and the force of the antichrist. It's the battle for the church, and it's one of the End-Time signs that will hit closest to home with Christians.

> *But mark this: There will be terrible times in the last days. People will be lovers of themselves, lovers of money, boastful, proud, abusive, disobedient to their parents, ungrateful, unholy, without love, unforgiving, slanderous, without self-control, brutal, not lovers of the good, treacherous, rash, conceited, lovers of pleasure rather than lovers of God— having a form of godliness but denying its power. Have nothing to do with them. They are the kind who worm their way into homes and gain control over weak-willed women, who are loaded down with sins and are swayed by all kinds of evil*

The Battle for the Church

desires, always learning but never able to acknowledge the truth.

—2 Timothy 3:1–9

That's what the Bible says will mark the End Times. Are we seeing these negative character traits more and more frequently? Yes, we are. The Bible says things are going to get even worse—but it also states that it's the church and not Babylon that holds the key to the future. As things get worse—and they're going to—the church will shine brighter as a beacon to the lost and hurting. As the world gets darker—and it's going to—the church will shine brighter as the place where eternal answers, peace, love, and hope can be found. If you liken the End Times to a hurricane, then the church would be the eye—the center, where there is peace in the midst of the storm. Storm winds and hurricane gales may swirl around the perimeter, but inside the eye are peace, tranquillity, and safety. The church is where the action is going to be. . . .

WHO IS THE CHURCH?

The church is the people of God. It is composed of every Christian, everywhere, at all times. Every Christian on earth today is a part of the living church. Whether or not we attend the same local church is not even an issue. The issues are these: Do we worship the same Christ as the One who was born of a woman, the Son of God . . . the One who died, was resurrected, and will come again? Do we acknowledge that He is Jesus—the truth, the way, and the life, and the only door to heaven?

If your answer to each of these questions is yes, then you are a member of the church. The church is the focus of God's love and the reflection of His glory: "For God so loved the world He gave His one and only Son, that whoever believes in him shall not perish but have eternal life" (John 3:16). From this well-known scripture, we can see that God loves the world. But I would like to make a statement that is somewhat controversial by nature. I would like to propose that He loves the church even more than He loves the world. If you stop to think about what I'm saying for a minute, you'll probably agree that this idea is not as scandalous as it may at first sound.

I don't mean God doesn't love the world. I mean that there is a deeper, fuller love given to those who receive Jesus. Anyone who receives Him as Lord and Savior has a special place in the heart of God. Jesus has, after all, shared His destiny and His very life's blood with them. We can never imagine how deeply and fervently God loves His children. Paul prayed that we would have insight into this very thing, praying that we 'may have power, together with all the saints, to grasp how wide and long and high and deep is the love of Christ, and to know this love that surpasses knowledge" (Eph. 3:18–19).

Do you think it's prideful of me to believe such a thing? I'm sorry, but I don't think so. I believe God loved us when we were in sin; that's scriptural, and indicates His love for all mankind. But I also believe that when we became His sons and daughters, He gave us spiritual authority in the form of the power of His name and the power of His blood. And He gave us more—a spiritual inheritance that includes the right to rule and reign with Him.

The church is the focus of God's glory. It's not a building; it's you and me. We have the right to honor Him, serve Him, and bless Him, because the Bible says, "He predestined us to be adopted as His sons through Jesus Christ, in accordance with his pleasure and will—to the praise of his glorious grace, which he has freely given us in the One he loves" (Eph. 1:5–6). We alone have been given the privilege of bringing honor, praises, and glory to God through our lives. We reflect Him. We honor Him. We love Him. And He loves us back.

> *Now unto him that is able to do exceeding abundantly above all that we ask or think, according to the power that worketh in us, unto him be glory in the church by Christ Jesus throughout all ages, world without end. Amen. I, therefore, the prisoner of the lord, beseech you that ye walk worthy of the vocation wherewith ye were called.*
>
> —Ephesians 3:20–4:1, KJV

◆ ◆ ◆

WHAT IS THE CHURCH?

The church is the instrument of God's will in the earth. It is the instrument by which God's will is done and victory over Satan is eventually achieved. It's the place where the eternal battle between good and evil will be fought and the location of the struggle for the souls of mankind. All this will be focused through us—Christians—in these last days because the battle is on. And we must be ready.

> *Finally, my brethren, be strong in the Lord and in the power of His might. Put on the whole armor of God, that you may be able to stand against the wiles of the devil. For we do not wrestle against flesh and blood, but against principalities, against powers, against the rulers of the darkness of this age, against spiritual hosts of wickedness in the heavenly places.*
>
> —Ephesians 6:10–13, NKJV

As I have already mentioned, the church is the key to the End-Time struggle between God and Satan. In order for the enemy to do his work on earth—to spread his deceptive influence—he must first deal with the church. We resist him and actually hold him back from running rampantly across the planet, performing whatever evil he wishes. We are the one thing standing between the enemy and his goal of world domination. That's an awesome thought, isn't it?

The Battle for the Church

Satan knows you and I have the right and the power to bring God glory. That's why he attacks us so viciously. He has to deal with you and me in order to get to God. He has to overcome us in order to overcome the world. As the church goes, so goes the world. The apostle Paul wrote, "Don't you remember that when I was with you I used to tell you these things? And now you know what is holding him [Satan] back, so that he may be revealed at the proper time. For the secret power of lawlessness is already at work; but the one who now holds it back will continue to do so till he is taken out of the way. And then the lawless one will be revealed, whom the Lord Jesus will overthrow with the breath of his mouth and destroy by the splendor of His coming" (2 Thess. 2:5–8).

Can you see the significance of the church? Satan's work on earth is limited, because something is at all times resisting him, and that "something" is the church. It's not that he doesn't want to establish his evil empire right now; it's that he can't. He can't because he's being stopped. And we're the ones stopping him.

The Holy Spirit moving through the church is who is stopping him, to be specific. The Holy Spirit built the church, and He is the One filling it. There is no church without the Holy Spirit. There is no life without the Holy Spirit. When the Holy Spirit is gone, we're in big trouble. I'll talk about that later.

IN THE MEANTIME . . .

In the meantime . . . we're under pressure. We're under pressure because we're the ones resisting Satan and the ones he has to deal with on earth. That's why we're under such a load of pressure, serving God. It ought to be easier than it is, but it's hard—and getting harder.

Why is it that we wrestle with such powerful unseen forces, just to win the right to love and serve God? Because we're caught in warfare. We're in the midst of war every day, like it or not, whether or not we're even aware of it. Satan knows he has to deal with us in order to take over the town. And if he takes the town, he'll take the county . . . and then the state . . . the nation . . . and the world.

That's why we must continue to resist the enemy. We're all that stands between Satan and the world. Remember what he wants—has always wanted. He wants to be worshiped, as God is worshiped. He wants a following—has to have a crowd—or he's not interested. So if he can't get a person into actual satanic worship, he'll take the next best thing—worship via the counterfeit one-world religion. And if he can't have that, he'll settle for third choice—to neutralize Christians in their efforts to serve and worship God. At the very least, he wants to paralyze Christians and make their lives powerless.

◆ ◆ ◆

The Battle for the Church

The Bible tells us specifically that in the last days, there will be visible spiritual changes in the lives of Christians. For one thing, there will be a major falling away from the faith. "Let no one deceive you by any means; for that Day will not come unless the falling away comes first, and the man of sin is revealed, the son of perdition" (2 Thess. 2:3, NKJV). "And because lawlessness will abound, the love of many will grow cold" (Matt. 24:12, NKJV). *Apostasy* is the New Testament term for this falling away; in the Old Testament, it was known as "backsliding." Both are words to describe the defection from truth, or turning aside from the way of God. The concept of apostasy is similar to that of divorce—it means to actually lose touch with or to become separated in relationship from God.

This is no minor thing. In fact, the Bible says there will be a tidal wave of change involving the condition of the hearts of previously zealous Christians. Their hearts will grow cold. Many shall be deceived. They'll stop loving and serving God and will be turned aside en masse to Satan's subtle agenda—an agenda that involves more than just their individual lives. It involves the whole planet.

This great falling away will be the result of increased evil and last-day deception. The day He dropped the prophecy bomb, Jesus warned: "Watch out that no one deceives you. For many will come in my name, claiming, 'I am the Christ,' and will deceive many" (Matt. 24:4–5). He then addresses this great falling away: "At that time many will turn away from the faith and will betray and hate each other, and many false prophets will appear and deceive many people" (Matt. 24:10–11).

Who was Jesus addressing at the time He dropped the prophecy bomb? His disciples. He was talking to those closest to Him, those who had walked with Him and talked with Him for three-and-a-half years. They knew Him best, yet these He warned, "Watch out! Many of you will be deceived. No one is exempt from this widespread deception. Many will turn away from the faith and even begin to hate each other. Watch out!"

It's a little like waiting around to see how many of those who begin college actually complete their course work. I recall an instructor telling me and my classmates at the beginning of a premed chemistry class, "Two-thirds of you will not be here in two years." I remember thinking, *You poor suckers,* as I looked around the classroom. Guess who was one of those two-thirds? *Moi.*

No one is exempt; it could happen to anyone because "your enemy the devil prowls around like a roaring lion looking for someone to devour" (1 Pet. 5:8).

Can you understand the seriousness of this? It means that many of those you're walking with right now will not be around to finish the race with you. And all because they were deceived. A deceived person believes he or she is right. Just as we who believe in Christ believe we're right, the Hindu believes he is right, and the Muslim believes he is right, and the New Ager believes he is right, and the Jehovah's Witness believes he is right, and the Mormon believes he is right. So how does anyone know who is right for sure?

Deception is another word for "seduction," which means "to lead away or to entice." Why is deception such a powerful weapon to unleash against the church? Because it's not a direct, frontal attack. Deception is often so subtle in nature as to go unnoticed and therefore unchecked until much damage has been done. If, for instance, the devil would prance around with horns unsheathed and pitchfork in hand, we'd have no trouble recognizing him. However, he rarely does that. He comes disguised as something else—something good—and we buy in more easily that way.

If he were obvious, no one would be deceived. So he's not obvious. He comes wearing an expensive pinstripe suit and silk tie, carrying a top-grain leather Bible, and looking good. He blends in, gains our confidence, confuses us, then leads some away with his smooth-sounding religious rhetoric. This deception will have a significant impact in causing many to depart from the faith.

The question is, how can we know for certain who is telling the truth? And if there's so much deception out there, how on earth will we ever recognize these subtle spiritual attacks? Let me share with you ten major things you can look for as Satan steps up his assault against the church:

1. REJECTION

There will come a time when it is so unpopular to be a Christian and there is so much hatred unleashed against believers that they will actually be mocked and rejected just for their faith. Some may even be killed. "Then you will be handed over to be persecuted and put to death, and you will be hated by all nations because of me" (Matt. 24:9). This scripture is being fulfilled around us every day, and as we move further into the End Times, this will only increase. Society at large—the secularists—already seem to hate what God is doing on earth in this hour. Not too long ago I heard about a couple who were kicked out of the church they'd attended for years because the woman claimed to have received the miracle of divine healing. Representatives of her church even stated, "We know it was a miracle but we don't have room for miracles here; therefore you must leave."

That couple was persecuted because of their belief in a healing God of miracles instead of a silent God who no longer performs them. Who would believe such a dangerous thing? Who, indeed! Would it surprise you to know that the secular world's assessment of most evangelicals is that they're "ignorant, gullible, and dangerous to society"? That's what an article in the *Washington Post* stated. When evangelicals began to phone the newspaper with their bitter complaints, the response was: "We just thought it was common knowledge." *Rejection.* It's out there. And it's going to get worse.

2. CONFLICT WITHIN THE CHURCH

"At that time many will turn away from the faith and will betray and hate each other" (Matt. 24:10). It's clear from this passage of text that Christians will begin to turn on each other. The next front of spiritual attack will be from within. The day Jesus dropped the prophecy bomb, the disciples thought such a thing to be unthinkable. "No way! We're family!" But Jesus said, "Think again. The time will come when you'll fight and hate and persecute each other." He was right. It's already happening, and it's going to get worse.

3. OFFENSE

Being overly sensitive is another End-Time sign that will crop up when Christians get under pressure. Matthew 24:10 states, "And then shall many be offended, and shall betray one another, and shall hate one another" (KJV). In this instance, the word *offend* means "to trip up, to set up for a fight, to try to bring another one down." It also means "to remove joy," or to take the joyfulness from serving Christ. Can you see that happening? I can see it, and it will increase.

4. THE LOSS OF SPIRITUAL PASSION

The battle for the believer's passion for Christ and others will be one of the central End-Time spiritual battles. Can I be honest with you? I am passionate about Christ. But in the past few years I have been appalled at how difficult it is to keep my passion for Jesus alive and well amid all the distractions and the pressures of daily living. It's never been this intense. I have to work harder and stay more focused in order to keep my spiritual edge. Can anybody identify? "And because lawlessness will abound, the love of many will grow cold" (Matt. 24:12, NKJV). As one's love for Christ grows cold, it results in a loss of spiritual passion. And spiritual passion is vital, for without it, we become drained until we're empty. Then we fall away.

5. A TIME OF SAVAGERY

People are going to be increasingly hard to deal with in the End Times—fierce, violent, harsh, and competitive. Second Timothy, chapter 3 warns us that people will become "without love, unforgiving, slanderous, without self-control, brutal, not lovers of the good" (v. 3). Verse 4 goes on to describe this new breed of people as "treacherous, rash, and conceited." Not very good traits to find in people. But it's happening now, and it's going to get worse because it's going to be happening among Christians. If I had five dollars for every Christian who said he was unwilling to forgive another Christian, I'd be a wealthy man. I could retire. Who would have thought twenty years ago that the day would come when Christians refused to forgive?

6. SELF-FOCUSED

How many times do we hear this question: "Yes, but how will it affect me?" Who cares. We're all called, as Christians, to lay down our personal agendas and pick up the cross of Christ. Is that even being taught anymore? Instead, Christians have joined the "me generation" and become self-centered and out for what they can get. "What's in it for me?" has become a kind of battle cry but not the one that will win this spiritual battle in the End Times.

7. IRRELIGIOUS

It's all around us, this mocking of religious themes and carefully cloaked blasphemy. Christian symbols, standards, and lifestyles are steadily under attack. One day soon they'll be so eroded that even Christians will partake of the seemingly harmless irreligious repartee. No respect, no fear of God, no honor, no reverence for Him—another End-Time sign of the subtle attack waged against the church.

8. PLEASURE ADDICTION

This addiction is more than just loving to have more. Pleasure addiction is a surrender to the superfluous, the shallow, and the nonessential. It will take a Christian under pretty quickly. For at its root is not the pursuit of pleasure but the unwillingness to see life and its purpose for what it is—the sovereign property of God. In pursuing pleasure and not God, we are subtly saying, "I choose the superficial and not the deep."

9. POWERLESS CHRISTIANITY

All form . . . no substance . . . toothless Christianity. This is the era for these things, and Satan is stepping up his efforts to get Christians where he wants them—harmless and "having a form of godliness but denying its power. Have nothing to do with them" (2 Tim. 3:5). Now more than ever, it's important for us as Christians to differentiate the real from the fake, the showy exterior from the interior deeps. We must get beyond all the attention paid to the outward appearance and learn to spot, then major on, the condition of the heart. We must allow the Holy Spirit to take us deeper, so that we are transformed by His presence in our lives and conformed to the image of Christ. We must be wary of the enemy's attempts to get us over into religious form, where there is no substance, and we must be vigilant about the essentials of the faith that keep the power flowing from the Source—the throne of God.

10. DIFFUSION OF TRUTH

These End Times will be marked by a loss of sound doctrine, as the foundations of the faith are continually bombarded with compromise and the deceptive assaults of the enemy. "For the time will come when men will not put up with sound doctrine. Instead, to suit their own desires, they will gather around them a great number of teachers to say what their itching ears want to hear. They will turn their ears away from the truth and turn aside to myths" (2 Tim. 4:3–4). Jesus said there will be a flood of false prophets and false doctrines. Some churches tolerate this and even teach them. It's tragic, but many of our families are having the truth of the gospel diffused by mixture with false doctrines, and these will lead to their falling away from the faith.

The Battle for the Church

11. SPIRITUAL BURNOUT

This is the number-one hit against the church, I'm convinced. It's real, just like career burnout. And it's not the disease of the lukewarm or the unconcerned. It's the disease of the intensely passionate—the fervent ones, the dreamers and the doers. After all, there must first be a fire in order for one to burn out. I can think of a number of examples from the Bible of those who suffered burnout: Elijah, Solomon, King Saul, David, the entire nation of Israel. Jesus didn't say spiritual burnout was the result of not loving Him, but of what we see around us: evil out of control, an overwhelming amount of work to be done and not enough willing workers to roll up their sleeves and do it.

Those things are what can lead to spiritual burnout. When we overextend ourselves and our resources, when we become isolated and self-sufficient, when we allow ourselves to become over-sensitive, when we have unrealistic expectations and goals, we burn out. The wounds we leave unattended and the needs that aren't met will leave us tired and bitter and just burned out. Busyness will burn us out. So will the loss of hope. Some of the symptoms of spiritual burnout are irritability, criticalness, judging, and pointing out the flaws of others; spiritual weariness, when it becomes a struggle to even pray and read the Bible; loss of courage and withdrawing from spiritual challenges; an absence of Christ's love and acceptance; a negative mental attitude; withdrawal from fellowship with other Christians; loss of objectivity. Spiritual burnout has serious consequences because it is one of these subtle fronts of spiritual warfare. Unchecked, it can cause even the most passionate Christian to simply fall away.

SO WHAT CAN WE DO ABOUT THESE SPIRITUAL ATTACKS?

You don't have to sit there and take it; there are some things you can do to keep from going under spiritually. The Bible says we win!

Here are some practical things to do that may help you last until the end and win:

• DON'T PANIC!

I've said it before, and I'll say it again—don't panic, because panic plays right into the enemy's hand. Fear will cut your faith and increase the power of the enemy's attack. So stay cool, don't panic, and keep your spiritual perspective.

• BE SPIRITUAL.

I don't mean on the outside—I mean bonedeep. To be truly, genuinely spiritual is to be in tune with the Holy Spirit and His work through you on earth. He dwells in you, as the believer, and the more closely you learn to walk with Him and lean solely on Him, the more genuinely spiritual you will become. Stop trying to look like, act like, and conform to the world. Carnal Christianity has no power, only excuses and demands. It's not just

The Battle for the Church

powerless; it's dangerous, especially in the End Times. The Bible says that to be carnally minded is death; to be spiritually minded is life by the Holy Spirit. Live life according to God's perspective, and not only will you find yourself becoming truly spiritual but you will also find yourself becoming truly powerful in the Holy Spirit.

- *BE ACTIVE.*

An amazing strength is given to those who move forward in ministry. They are empowered by the Holy Spirit to do more than is physically possible in and of themselves. In God's kingdom, strength comes from right involvement, not from withdrawal. Staying active in Christian fellowship empowers the Christian to keep on going and to do more, not less, for God's kingdom. What will keep you moving forward is to be proactive—to be active and passionate about God's will for the world. That means proclaiming the gospel and standing for Christ, even if it means doing so in the midst of pressure and persecution, difficulties and setbacks. God's people will not just survive against these assaults; they'll win.

- *BE DETERMINED.*

You will win if you endure. This is a word of encouragement from Christ for every Christian. Endurance is the one common denominator of every Christian, in every church, in every age. What does it mean to endure? It means to stay when you really feel like quitting. It means to realize that what we're doing for God really matters, and makes a difference, even when it does not seem evident at the time. It means to know that Christianity works, and that in the end we win. When we know these things, we can endure. We are not fighting a losing battle. God promises that we can do it—and we can. What we stand for is worth the effort—at any cost. It's too valuable and important to abandon. The church is not some out-of-date, useless organization to be cast off and forsaken in her hour of need. The church, the body of Christ, holds the keys to the End Times, and we shall rule and reign with Christ when He returns. Until then, let's hold fast and endure.

- *BE CHRIST'S.*

Be true to Jesus. Victory in the End Times will come to those who sign up 100 percent for Jesus Christ and become His and His alone. Everything about the faith boils down to that one thing. Serving Christ will cost you something in the last days. It's not going to be popular to serve Christ. There will be persecution, rejection, warfare, weariness, and resistance. Be Christ's, and He will get you through. Jesus said, "I am the way, the truth, and the life: no man cometh unto the father, but by me" (John 14:6, KJV). "Verily, verily, I say unto you, Except a corn of wheat fall into the ground and die, it abideth alone: but if it die, it bringeth forth much fruit. He that loveth his life shall lose it; and he that hateth his life in this world shall keep it unto life eternal. If any man serve me, let him follow me; and where I am, there shall also my servant be: if any man serve me, him will my father honor" (John 12:24–26, KJV). Sell out to Jesus. Follow Him! Fervent, committed Christianity is not brainless or lifeless. Serving Christ does not mean that we have no life; it simply means that He comes first and gives us life abundantly.

• *BE POWERFUL.*

Christ has called us to be more than just dedicated; He has called us to be powerful. We must have the power of the Holy Spirit in order to stand strong in the End Times. He is our strength in the hard places of life. Be empowered by the Holy Spirit. Be lifted by the resurrection power of Jesus Christ above the hardness and the darkness all around us. Shine in the darkness. "Finally, be strong in the Lord and in his mighty power" (Eph. 6:10).

• *BE KIND.*

The spirit of Christ is the spirit of love. Love overcomes hatred and judgment. We must always remember that people are not our enemies; the spirit of the world and our adversary the devil are our true enemies. We must be absolutely, uncompromisingly Christian, but we must also be kind. There are a lot of well-meaning people in the church today who miss it on this one point. They spend time dividing doctrinal hairs, then get touchy with their fellow Christians who see things differently than they do. They become offended and then mean-spirited.

We must learn to appreciate the good and to love our brothers and sisters in Christ, agreeing on the common ground of core Christian issues and minoring on the small stuff. We must be able to listen and when the opportunity arises, sow a seed now and then under the inspiration of the Holy Spirit. Also, think about this for a minute: Not everyone who does not love Christ is a bad person. Not all non-Christians are evil. They are wrong on the most important issue of life. But they are not necessarily evil. So to treat them as if they are, and not to treat them kindly, is our serious mistake. Let's walk in love. Let's be kind. Let's love as Christ loved us, and if necessary be willing to lay down our lives for our friends.

• *BE LOYAL.*

This is the hour of absolute commitment to Christ, not of lukewarm Christianity. To be loyal means to come out of the system of Babylon and the system of the world and commit every area of our lives—from economics, to our personal lives, to our lives in fellowship with other Christians—to the Lord. Jesus must be Lord over all. You can have non-Christian friends but keep your Christian edge so that you can witness to the world.

Staying separate and refusing to fellowship with nonbelievers is not what I'm talking about; I'm talking about compromise. Don't do it! Be willing to jettison anything that drags you down and keeps you from 100 percent commitment to Christ.

The Battle for the Church

We must draw the line when any organization, any person, any church, or any family member asks us to compromise our faith in Him. We must not compromise—not to succeed and not even to help others. And by that, I mean that we can disagree with someone and still keep contact with that person. But if that person begins to exert pressure to get us into compromise, that's the time to draw the line.

When the issues of salvation through Christ alone and His position as only begotten, risen Son of God are threatened with compromise, that's where you must stand fast. Be loyal to Christ, and it will help you hold fast when the temptation to compromise hits.

◆ ◆ ◆

SURVIVAL IN THE "SELF" GENERATION

We've heard it called the "me" generation, or the "self" generation. More than any other time in history, this generation is consumed with "what's in it for me?" One of the byproducts of this self generation is the idea that we can select for ourselves what to believe and what not to believe as if it were our right to cut-and-paste our way into universal truth. Some of us alive today have bought into age-old spiritual error dressed up to look like advanced new concepts. Thus, people in droves admit they no longer know what to believe.

The researcher and pollster, George Barna, has kept his finger on the pulse of the public pertaining to spiritual matters for the last few decades. He observes, "We expect more of others than we allow them to demand of us. . . . We respond to opportunities in life on the basis of what works best for us, at the moment, without reference to the impact of our decisions upon others or upon our own long-term future."

We don't think; we act. This has produced a generation of people who limp through life, having trouble with commitment issues, drifting with the tides of culture. Is it any wonder that 92 percent of Americans say they believe in God, but only one-third say they have made a personal commitment to Jesus Christ, trusting in God rather than their own best efforts to get them through life. Only another third of that one-third say they believe it's important to maintain that personal relationship with Christ through a daily commitment to prayer and Bible study.

Of those Barna surveyed, 84 percent said religion was very important in their lives. However, only 20 percent said they made decisions based on God's value system. Thirty-six percent said they believed Jesus made mistakes, yet the majority indicated that they believed Him to be the Son of God.

Go figure.

Sixty-two percent of born-again Christians said they did not believe there was such a thing as absolute truth. And according to the survey, the highest goal in life as expressed by most of the respondents was "self-actualization and a better lifestyle." Seventy-three percent of Americans said the main purpose of life was to enjoy it and to achieve personal fulfillment.

The Battle for the Church

Whatever happened to the cross?

It's a battle. The battle for the church. If we're to stay strong and not become weak and wandering in the way, we're going to have to roll up our sleeves and fight!

After God determines that this battle for the church has been waged long enough, the next great event of the future will take place: the Rapture!

6

THE RAPTURE

et me tell you why I believe the Rapture is going to occur before the seven-year period of hell on earth that the Bible calls the Tribulation. While there are a number of possibilities as to the timing of the Rapture, here's why I believe the Rapture will take place sooner not later. The Bible states that before the Tribulation really cranks up, the Holy Spirit will be taken out of the earth. The Holy Spirit is the only force on earth strong enough to restrain the forces of Satan. How does the Holy Spirit operate on earth today? Through the people of God—through Christians. Therefore, it stands to reason that if the Holy Spirit is to be entirely removed out of the earth and rescinded to heaven, then we're going to have to go right along up with Him.

Of course, many dedicated, sincere Christians do not share my views concerning the Rapture and when it may occur. Rather than focusing on the points where we may disagree, I would rather focus on those points we, as believers, agree on. After all, the real issue is this: Jesus is coming soon. Be ready!

While the word *rapture* does not come up again and again in Scripture, the concept of the rapture does. The word *rapture* means "to be caught away." One day we shall be caught away heavenward to be with the Lord. I would like to make the distinction immediately between the Rapture and the return of Christ. These are two separate events and are not to be confused for one-and-the-same.

CAUGHT UP TOGETHER . . . IN THE CLOUDS

This is what the Bible says:

> *According to the Lord's own word, we tell you that we who are still alive, who are left till the coming of the Lord, will certainly not precede those who have fallen asleep. For the Lord himself will come down from heaven, with a loud command, with the voice of the archangel and with the trumpet call of God, and the dead in Christ will rise first. After that, we*

The Rapture

who are still alive and are left will be caught up with them in the clouds to meet the Lord in the air. And so we will be with the Lord forever. . . . The day of the Lord will come like a thief in the night. While people are saying, "Peace and safety," destruction will come on them suddenly, as labor pains on a pregnant woman, and they will not escape.

But you, brothers, are not in darkness so that this day should surprise you like a thief. You are all sons of the light and sons of the day. . . . But since we belong to the day, let us be self-controlled, putting on faith and love as a breastplate, and the hope of salvation as a helmet. For God did not appoint us to suffer wrath but to receive salvation through our Lord Jesus Christ.

—1 Thessalonians 4:15–5:9

As it was in the days of Noah, so it will be at the coming of the Son of Man. For in the days before the flood, people were eating and drinking, marrying and giving in marriage, up to the day Noah entered the ark; and they knew nothing about what would happen until the flood came and took them all away. That is how it will be at the coming of the Son of Man. Two men will be in the field; one will be taken and the other left. Two women will be grinding with a hand mill; one will be taken and the other left.

Therefore keep watch, because you do not know on what day your Lord will come. But understand this: If the owner of the house had known at what time of night the thief was coming, he would have kept watch and would not have let his house be broken into. So you also must be ready, because the Son of Man will come at an hour when you do not expect him.

—Matthew 24:37–44

From these two passages of Scripture, we see several interesting points regarding the Rapture. In the verses from 1 Thessalonians, we see the Lord coming "as a thief in the night" to catch His children up with Him in the clouds. We see also that He "did not appoint us to suffer wrath but to receive salvation through our Lord Jesus Christ." What could be more wrathful than the Tribulation when the Holy Spirit departs earth and lawlessness reigns, unchecked, at the hands of the Antichrist? In the Matthew text, we see a separation taking place—a literal choosing between one and the other, as God separates His children and selects them, one by one. Again, He comes as a thief in the night, and as in the passage in 1 Thessalonians, we are told to be ready.

Many of you were raised in a church that taught about the Rapture. I was too. Can you recall the first time an event occurred that made you fear you may have missed the Rapture? Is there anything more frightening?

That moment came for me when I was about

The Rapture

fourteen. My family and I were traveling to Oklahoma from Ohio, and we stopped at a tiny rest stop. I was lagging behind, dragging my feet. Dad said, "Randal, you'd better hurry up, or we'll leave without you!" I kept right on, dragging my feet as usual. When I finally reached the car, no one was there. The car was right where I remembered that it had been parked, but it was empty. I was worried, but I didn't panic because the thought struck me that my family had probably just walked over to a nearby restaurant. So I sauntered over to the restaurant to check things out. I searched the serving area; my family was nowhere to be seen. I checked the men's room; nothing. I even cracked open the door of the ladies' room and shouted, "Mama!" No answer.

Now I was panicked.

Surely the Rapture hadn't occurred . . . had it? If it had, my teenage rebellion had kept me from going up with the rest of my family! I broke out in a cold sweat as I walked back over to the car and paced back and forth, back and forth, hands jammed into the pockets of my jeans. A very long half-hour later, my family returned to the car, laughing and cutting up with each other as if nothing at all were wrong. They told me they had walked across the road to see something. That harmless life episode made a very big impact on me, however, and I can't help thinking, each time I recall it, that this is how it will be on the day of the Rapture. Not scary at all, unless you miss going up.

You see, we're not meant to fear the Rapture; the Lord never intended for us to fear it or to find it confusing. He warned us to be ready. And if

we're ready for the Rapture, we have nothing at all
to fear.

THE SPECTACULAR EVENT OF THE END TIME

*There's nothing more spectacular, I'm convinced,
than the Rapture; nor has anything as much con-
sequence.* It has to be the most electrifying event
in the future of the church, since it's the day when
Christ Himself will announce His coming to His
faithful servants with a shout and a trumpet blast.
The Bible says that a shout signifies first the
Rapture, then His coming. The dead in Christ will
leave their graves, and those of us alive on earth
will rise to meet Him in the air. "And so we will be
with the Lord forever" (see 1 Thess. 4:16–17).

Don't you think that's good news? Yet a surprisingly large number of Christians claim to be
confused over this one issue; many others admit
they fear the Rapture. At the very least, they're disturbed at the thought they might miss it. Others
are agitated because they say they're not sure who
will get to go up in the Rapture and who will be
left behind. Imagine the chaos on earth on the day
of the Rapture, as some people are taken alive out
of the earth and others actually realize their
absence.

The next event after the Rapture will be nothing
less than the return of Christ. For centuries people
on earth have anxiously awaited that momentous
event. Take, for instance, the standing-room-only
crowd that crushed inside St. Peter's Basilica as

The Rapture

Pope Sylvester II led the congregation in hymns and prayers in advance of what all believed would be the return of Christ. Hysteria gripped the crowd as the people dropped to their knees or fell prostrate in prayer as the Pope proclaimed: "This is the final hour, the beginning of the days of wrath, the nightfall of the universe."

At the same time in Jerusalem, hundreds of thousands of pilgrims milled about in mass hysteria, flocking to the spot where they expected Jesus to return—the Mount of Olives. At any moment, they expected to see Him descend from the clouds. All across Europe, people had donated lands, homes, and goods to the poor in final acts of contrition. Debts had been canceled, infidelities confessed, and wrongdoings forgiven en masse. Businesses were neglected, buildings were left vacant and in disrepair, and fields were left dormant and uncultivated while churches were jammed with crowds seeking absolution of their sins. The most sincere believers roamed the countryside, whipping one another in penance and mortification.

All these acts led up to New Years Eve, A.D. 999, when at midnight Pope Sylvester II raised his arms heavenward and began to sing the Te Deum. The crowd scarcely dared to breathe; an eyewitness recorded, "not a few died from fright, giving up their ghosts then and there." These outbreaks of panic and mass terror occurred among Christians. But Jesus did not return on the night of the dawning of the new millennium.

What was meant to inspire and motivate Christians, what was meant to fill believers with joy and expectation has instead, throughout history, been wrongly interpreted as a cause of fear and hysteria.

Take, for instance, what happened in March 1809: Mary Mateman of York, England, said her brown hen was laying "Rapture eggs" that predicted both the Rapture and return of Christ. "Today you will witness a miracle," she said, "by which we are warned that the end of the world is at hand and that our dead savior is about to come in clouds of glory to begin His final reign on earth." Suddenly, amid much angry cackling, her brown hen would produce an egg. The curious could examine the "Rapture egg," for a fee, mind you, and see that written clearly across each shell were the words, "Christ is coming." Suspecting chicanery, a doctor caught Mateman in the act of forcing an egg into the hens oviduct while the hen cackled menacingly. Nearby lay a pen and a bottle of ink. When the charlatanism was exposed, twenty thousand spectators saw her hanged for wrongly prophesying the Rapture.

In 1988 a retired NASA rocket engineer, Edgar C. Whisenhunt, published a little book entitled *88 Reasons Why Jesus Christ Will Come in 1988*. The self-published mini-book sold 4.5 million copies. When the Rapture and consequent return of Christ did not occur, as prophesied, he changed the name of the booklet to *The Final Shout Rapture Report, 1989*. But those who bought in at the beginning became disenchanted with his views, and the author who made headlines in the late eighties hasn't been heard from lately.

Just a few years ago, *Time* magazine reported

The Rapture

strange incidents that occurred in Seoul, South Korea. Forty-six-year-old Pastor Lee Jang Rim was sentenced to two years in prison for defrauding believers out of four million dollars by what the court termed "Rapture hysteria." His faithful followers had distributed flyers worldwide which read, "Rapture! 666 = Hell!" Fear, mockery, and debate rang out from California to Washington, D.C. as Rim and his followers proclaimed the Rapture was set to take place on October 28, 1992. The date came and went without incident—other than the thousands who left their jobs, dropped out of school, sold their houses, divorced their spouses, and went AWOL from the military. As midnight of the date passed into history, the South Korean government dispatched fifteen hundred riot police to offset another possible Jonestown-type reaction—mass suicide by the hysterical adherents.

These are just a few historical accounts of how Rapture hysteria has promoted not joy but fear, anxiety, confusion, and loss among the body of Christ. It is vital that we keep the right perspective about this event that was always meant to be a blessing.

To get and keep the right perspective, let me share the four popular views regarding the Rapture that most Christians have held throughout the centuries. And let me state that regardless of what view you determine to be the right one, you should always remember this: Whenever God chooses to send this End-Time event is irrelevant. The fact that you remain ready is what counts. And should the view you select as the right one turn out to be the wrong one, don't despair: the Lord promised that we humans would see "through a glass darkly" and would "know in part . . . and prophesy in part," but that the glorious day will come when we shall know for certain and see clearly from our eternal vantage point—heaven (see 1 Cor. 13:9).

FOUR RAPTURE VIEWS

Four views about the Rapture predominate among Christians. The word *rapture* is not specifically mentioned in the Bible. It is an English word given to illuminate the words *harpazo* in Hebrew, which means "catching away" and *parousia* in the Greek, which means "coming" and refers more to Jesus' return. If the Rapture is being taught in your church, that teaching will probably follow along one of these lines:

1. PRETRIBULATION

Proponents of this view believe that the Rapture will occur prior to the Tribulation—that seven-year period on earth when the Holy Spirit will be taken out of the earth and evil will be allowed to run rampant, unchecked. The Antichrist will be at the helm during this period of darkness and deception. Pretribulationists believe that Christians won't experience the Tribulation, because the Rapture will take them out of the earth before the Tribulation begins. They believe that Christ will appear in the sky to meet raptured Christians, but that He will not set foot on earth until the Second Coming, which occurs at the end of the Tribulation seven years later (see 1 Thess. 4). According to this theory, many good religious people—but not true believers—will be left behind in the Rapture. Non-Christians will also be left behind. Only those born-again believers who have remained alert and stayed ready spiritually will go. There are a few side issues to this theory worth mentioning: first, if you miss the Rapture, there is no second chance. Those who do will go through the Tribulation, a time when committed Christians will die as martyrs and be welcomed into heaven, where they join those believers who have been raptured and those who believed throughout history. The biblical foundation of this theory can be found in 1 Thessalonians, chapter 4; Daniel, chapters 7 through 9; Ezekiel, chapters 38 and 39; Revelation, chapters 6 through 21; Matthew 24:38; and others.

The key concept to this theory of the Rapture is God's grace. Its proponents believe that God is too merciful to pour His full wrath out on earth while believers remain behind. Thus, in His measure to save Christians from His wrath, He must lift them out of the earth via the Rapture. We are saved from wrath by the blood of Christ. The Bible tells us "to wait for His Son from heaven, whom He raised from the dead, even Jesus who delivers us from the wrath to come" (1 Thess. 1:10, NKJV).

Pretribulationists believe that the grace of God is sufficient, and that the blood of Christ covers us and saves us from the time of God's wrath. Many pretribulationists believe that while one cannot know for certain exactly when the Rapture will occur, one can closely estimate by studying prophetic scripture passages such as Daniel's End-Time visions. That's why many pretribulationists study prophetic passages so closely; they want to be ready. They don't take for granted living for Christ daily. They don't want to be found sleeping and miss the Rapture. On the other hand, this view can lead to pessimism and other extremes. Some pretribulationists become so absorbed in their theological views that they withdraw from society and adopt the "bad days are coming" perspective, becoming caught up in identifying signs of the times versus the hands-on End-Time work of Christ on earth and with advancing the gospel to the lost.

2. MIDTRIBULATION

This second view states that the Rapture will come at some midway point during the Tribulation. In other words, believers will go through at least half the Tribulation before the trumpet blows. Why midway? Because the church is not ready to go; she is still being purified and dealt with spiritually. This view gives the church a time of purification and supports the scriptural idea that Christians would be persecuted; Christ, in fact, said so. Further, He told His disciples that "unless those days were shortened, no flesh would be saved; but for the elect's sake those days will be shortened" (Matt. 24:22, NKJV). According to this view, Christ is coming for a purified, spotless church, so we are called as Christians to experience something of a cleansing and preparation before we can go up.

The Rapture

3. POSTTRIBULATION

This theory says that the Rapture will take place at the end of the Tribulation and that, in short, Christians will go through it—all of it. The Christians will go up when the Rapture takes place at the end of the seven-year Tribulation, then come right back with Christ when He returns to earth shortly after the Rapture. Proponents of this End-Time view believe Christians will endure the reign of the Antichrist, famine, persecution, and war.

Posttribulationists tend to be far more zealous than most Christians, especially pretribulationists. Can you guess why? Because pretribulationists get to go up by grace; midtribulationists get to go up after they have been made pure; but posttribulationists believe they must be strong enough to stand against evil incarnate on earth. Further, they believe about those who hold these other views: "You're not going up like you think you are. Sooner or later you will believe what I believe, because you're going to be right here with me—and I will be able to tell you 'I told you so!'" Posttribulationists have it made, because if pretribulationists like myself are correct, then the posttribulationists get to go early.

The posttribulational theory, too, has many side issues. First, the Rapture occurs after the seven-year Tribulation, so the Rapture and Second Coming are almost simultaneous. This means that either both events occur at the same time, or Christians will go up only to come right back again. Many scriptures support this theory, including

Luke 17:30–37; 1 Thessalonians 4:13–18 and 30; and Revelation 1:7. Two key texts are found in the Book of Matthew: "At that time the sign of the Son of Man will appear in the sky, and all the nations of the earth will mourn. They will see the Son of Man coming on the clouds of the sky, with power and great glory. And he will send his angels with a loud trumpet call, and they will gather his elect from the four winds, from one end of the heavens to the other" (Matt. 24:30–31).

The other supports the idea that Christ will gather His people at the end of the Tribulation and that everyone will see it "when the Son of Man comes in his glory, and all the angels with him, he will sit on his throne in heavenly glory. . . . Then the king will say to those on his right, 'Come, you who are blessed by my Father; take your inheritance, the kingdom prepared for you since the creation of the world" (Matt. 25:31, 34).

The posttribulational view is the most ancient, historical view. It's what the early church believed, and it corresponds with many scripture passages throughout the Bible. For example, the Book of Revelation refers to the presence of all believers in all points of the Tribulation. An advantage to this view is that it helps people prepare for the worst possible scenario. There are also many dangers: One is that many who hold this view tend to become pessimistic and to withdraw from life. They tend to tune out the rest of the world and center just on getting themselves and their families ready to go through a horrible worldwide ordeal. After all, when you consider that you may have to go through the Tribulation, a time when two-thirds of the earth's population will probably be wiped out by fire or starvation or some other horror, the tendency is to have a pretty bleak outlook on life.

Posttribulationists tend to be more concerned with self-preservation than world evangelism. Some, however, are very positive and active regarding the promotion of the gospel. And this view does tend to make one extremely motivated to be ready to go when the Rapture does finally occur.

4. PARTIAL-RAPTURE

Those who hold this view believe that only those who are spiritually prepared and living for Christ with full hearts will be caught up in the Rapture. Those who don't go up on the first load will be left behind to go through the Tribulation and to get ready to meet Christ when He returns. A key text for this view is Revelation 2:21–23: "And I gave her time to repent of her sexual immorality, and she did not repent. Indeed I will cast her into a sickbed, and those who commit adultery with her into great tribulation, unless they repent of their deeds . . . And all the churches shall know that I am He who searches the minds and hearts. And I will give to each one of you according to your works" (NKJV). So what's the implication here? That it's possible that Christ will give people one last chance to repent. If they do not repent after being left behind in the Rapture, they will miss going to heaven to spend eternity with Him. Other texts in support of this view can be found in Matthew 25:13 and Matthew 25:30.

THE WRONG WAY TO AWAIT THE RAPTURE

Fear is the wrong attitude to have toward the Rapture; to live in panic is the wrong way to await this blessed event. I wanted you to have some idea of how Christians responded during these actual historic events because the fear expressed by the populace is an example of what we should not feel. We should feel excitement. We should eagerly look forward to that day. We should not be filled with fear and torment. That is not what Christ wanted for His people.

A pastor on my staff related to me the events that happened one night during a sleepover party for some teenagers. These thirteen- to sixteen-year-olds began talking about the End Times, and when someone said, "We are the last generation who will be here," the kids began to cry. All of them. In the end, all those crying kids lined up at an impromptu altar for prayer.

What was intended to be an encouragement in the End Times has become very frightening, not just to teenagers and children but also to adults. Those who are not yet Christians should be a little nervous about the Rapture and the return of Christ. But Christians should have no reason for anything but joy as these two final events approach. Yet Christians and non-Christians alike are living in fear at the mere mention of the Rapture and Christ's Second Coming.

The Rapture

The Rapture is responsible for sparking some of the most emotional of all eternal questions concerning religion: "Where has our view of the Rapture gone wrong?" "Why hasn't Christ come already, especially since the world is going to hell all around us?" "Will He return at all?" "If so, when?" "Who will get to go up in the Rapture?" "Who will be left behind?"

Jesus said we were not to be concerned with such matters. He Himself told the disciples, "Do not let your hearts be troubled. Trust in God, trust also in me. In my father's house are many rooms; if it were not so, I would have told you. I am going there to prepare a place for you. And if I go and prepare a place for you, I will come back and take you to be with me that you also may be where I am" (John 14:1–3).

Isn't that encouraging? We should also be encouraged to know that "we will all be changed—in a flash, in the twinkling of an eye, at the last trumpet. For the trumpet will sound, the dead will be raised imperishable, and we will be changed. For the perishable must clothe itself with the imperishable, and the mortal with immortality. When the perishable has been clothed with the imperishable, and the mortal with immortality, then the saying that is written will come true: 'Death has been swallowed up in victory'" (1 Cor. 15:51–54).

All four of these views share common scripture references which tell us to be ready. How do we do that? Let's see what the Bible has to say about it.

HOW TO BE READY

While we are not to fear the Rapture, we are to live in a state of readiness so that whenever it occurs, at whatever point in the End Times, we'll be ready to go. Here are some points to help us get ready and stay that way:

• **BE GROUNDED.**

Jesus told His disciples not to panic lest they miss the Big Picture. So regardless which of these views you adhere to, remember the point is not to know the false views or to major on all the verses about End-Time deception and the darkness all around. The point is to know the truth. Major on that, and you'll be grounded in the Word. If you don't know the truth, you'll have no standard with which to measure everything that deviates from it.

My biggest concern for the church is that even though we love God and attend church services, many of us don't even know the basics of Christianity. We need to know the truth and hold fast to it in these last days. It's vital that we understand the basics of grace, redemption, holiness, character, and the power of the Holy Spirit in order to know what is coming and how to handle it.

We must follow the Truth—Jesus. Don't follow crowds, and don't follow a charismatic personality. Follow Jesus. To do that, you must be grounded in the Word so that you know Him in the depths of your soul. In Matthew 24:23–27 Jesus said: "Then if any man shall say unto you,

The Rapture

Lo, here is Christ, or there; believe it not. For there shall arise false Christs, and false prophets, and shall show great signs and wonders; insomuch that, if it were possible, they shall deceive the very elect. Behold, I have told you before. Wherefore if they shall say unto you, behold, he is in the desert; go not forth: Behold, he is in the secret chambers, believe it not. For as the lightning cometh out of the east, and shineth even unto the west; so shall also the coming of the son of man be" (KJV). Only those who are grounded will be able to differentiate deception from truth, and resist the lie.

- *BE ALERT.*

Jesus told us, "Therefore keep watch, because you do not know on what day your Lord will come. But understand this: If the owner of the house had known at what time of night the thief was coming, he would have kept watch and would not have let his house be broken into. So you also must be ready, because the Son of Man will come at an hour when you do not expect him" (Matt. 24:42–44). Jesus uses the word "watch" two times in this passage. Obviously it was an important fact for us to note. We must remain vigilant and alert because as the End Times progress there will be the tendency to become groggy and drowsy. Our minds will be attacked with all sorts of distractions. We must fight to stay awake and remain watchful, not drifting into sleepiness and inactivity. We must remain on guard at our posts, so when the time comes we'll be ready.

Read again the parable of the foolish and wise virgins (see Matt. 25:5–13). Some were awake when the lord came for his bride; some had fallen asleep. Those who had fallen asleep were left behind, with a reprimand, "I tell you the truth, I don't know you." What can we learn from this parable? Three things—some things cannot be done at the last minute because a continual state of preparation must be maintained; some things cannot be borrowed, like oil for our spiritual lamps; some things will come upon us quickly, and thus we must remain ready.

Guard against the distractions sent upon the body of Christ by the spirit of the age—including too much activity, too many choices of things to do with our time, too much cynicism generated by all the bad news we take in daily, and the tendency to be flighty concerning the things of God. Don't get caught up in the wave of every prophetic craze; remain alert by keeping both feet on the ground, and, by all means, stay in the Word. The time to be on guard is when it appears that everything is going good and nothing much is happening. When you least expect Him, that's when the Lord will come.

• *BE EXPECTANT.*

Learn to live expectantly regarding the future, because Christ is your "hope of glory" (Col. 1:27). Joyful expectancy will both renew you and empower you during the difficult days ahead. There are all sorts of things tugging at us to gain our attention. Some of those things must be totally ignored. Some of those things must be attended to only in moderation. And some must be handled with one eye on Jesus and another on the task at hand.

Let's keep our focus firmly fixed on Him. Jesus said these days are not just about duty: These are exciting days, so we must keep our eyes on the blessed hope of Jesus Christ (see Titus 2:11–14). "For the grace of God that brings salvation has appeared to all men. It teaches us to say 'No' to ungodliness and worldly passions, and to live self-controlled, upright and godly lives in this present age, while we wait for the blessed hope—the glorious appearing of our great God and Savior, Jesus Christ, who gave himself for us to redeem us from all wickedness and to purify for himself a people that are his very own, eager to do what is good." That hope produces in us a joyful eager-ness. Jesus is saying, "Learn to maximize My joy in your lives. The harder the times, the more joy you will need. Don't allow End-Time pressures to take your joy from you."

Romans 8:18 states, "I consider that our present sufferings are not worth comparing with the glory that will be revealed in us." Remember, we are getting ready for a wedding party—not a funeral. So rejoice! There is a special reward to those who love His appearing: "Now there is in store for me the crown of righteousness, which the Lord, the righteous Judge, will award to me on that day—and not only to me, but also to all who have longed for His appearing" (2 Tim. 4:8). Be expectant! Eagerly await that day when He comes for us and we meet Him in the air!

- *BE ACTIVE.*

Continue to advance the kingdom on earth. Keep working to evangelize the lost. Stay active in church, because you will be blessed when the Master comes and finds you about His business. Matthew 24:45–51 states: "Who then is the faithful and wise servant, whom the master has put in charge of the servants in his household to give them their food at the proper time? It will be good for that servant whose master finds him doing so when he returns. I tell you the truth, he will put him in charge of all his possessions. But suppose that servant is wicked and says to himself, 'My master is staying away a long time,' and he then begins to beat his fellow servants and to eat and drink with drunkards. The master of that servant will come on a day when he does not expect him and at an hour he is not aware of. He will cut him to pieces and assign him a place with the hypocrites, where there will be weeping and gnashing of teeth."

The power of the Holy Spirit rests upon those who are busy and who stay focused on the things entrusted to them to do on earth. It's called proactive spirituality. The lie of hell is that retreating into yourself once you are saved is the best way— it's not. We are to go forward and share the gospel with the rest of the lost and dying world. We are to live victorious lives that are examples to the unsaved. We are to pray, witness, give, teach, help, and go. Spiritual activity is the secret ingredient of the vibrant, empowered, End-Time Christian. We must stay in fellowship, stay in ministry, and stay in forward motion.

The Rapture

So here are some things to do between now and the Rapture—practical things that will help you to get ready and stay ready. Because once the Rapture occurs, only one great End-Time event remains—the greatest of them all, the glorious return of Christ!

7

THE RETURN OF CHRIST

I t's the moment every Christian has been eagerly awaiting since Christ ascended to His Father after the Resurrection—His glorious return! It's been the source of debate and discussion down through the centuries and has sown division between differing factions who each believed their theological view to be the only right one. It has been the cause of false alarm, fear, and even division among the body of Christ. Some who believed He was coming at a certain time in history, on a particular day, became disillusioned and fell away from the faith when He did not appear as they expected.

The Second Coming—the final event in this series of seven coming events, *and the most glorious of all!* Anticipated throughout history, it is the one event that will draw mankind out of the clutches of the Antichrist and restore spiritual order and authority worldwide following the horrible seven-year Tribulation.

We await it with joy . . . don't we?

We should, but sadly some do not. Some fear it, find it confusing and wonder whether it will even happen. Of course it will happen. Jesus said it would.

So how do we as believers approach the return of Christ? How can we find joy if we currently aren't experiencing it? What do we do with the fear? How can we develop faith that will take us through the End Times to that wonderful day?

WHY THE SECOND COMING IS SO CONFUSING

In the New Testament, one verse out of every thirty pertains to Jesus' return. The coming of Christ is referred to either directly or indirectly more than five hundred times in the New Testament. "For the Lord Himself will come down from heaven, with a loud command, with the voice of the archangel and with the trumpet call of God, and the dead in Christ will rise first" (1 Thess. 4:16). Amazingly, almost 50 percent of Americans say they expect Christ to return and set up His earthly kingdom. Not surprisingly, however, there is a great deal of confusion and tremendous disagreement about how and when and under what circumstances He will return.

You would expect that something so important and so clearly delineated in Scripture, something predicted by Christ Himself and clarified further by His apostles would be universally agreed upon within the body of Christ. Not even close! Why not?

One reason for the confusion is the symbolic nature of apocalyptic scriptures. Scriptures in the prophetic books, such as Daniel and Revelation, are often clothed in symbolism. These books were written that way in order to protect the New Testament saints. So what do all these symbolic pictures mean? Which ones are to be taken literally and which ones are there for effect only? *You* figure it out.

Another reason for such a variety of theological opinions is that Christians often confuse the Second Coming with the Rapture, as I stated earlier. These are two different events, I again remind. Also, different calendars may be used to calculate a general date for Christ's return—the Roman calendar, the Jewish calendar, and the modern Gregorian calendar. Each of these calendars differs as much as several years from the other. So which of these calendars will God use when He determines it's time to send Christ to earth once again? Remember, Jesus was not trying to confuse us; He was trying to warn us, prepare us, and bless us on the day He dropped His prophecy bomb.

There are many godly and intelligent students of the Bible on each side of this great issue. Many good spiritual people believe different things, and we must not disregard the good we can gain from those who disagree with us on this important topic. As far as I'm concerned, as long as a person believes Jesus is coming again and that we must be ready for Him, then that person can't be too far offtrack. "Now, brothers, about times and dates we do not need to write to you, for you know very well that the day of the Lord will come like a thief in the night" (1 Thess. 5:1–2).

THREE VIEWS ON THE SECOND COMING OF CHRIST

Three theological views about the Second Coming of Christ predominate among believers. They are:

• *PREMILLENNIAL*

Proponents of this view believe that the Second Coming of Christ will occur before the millennial reign of Christ on earth. They contend that things will get worse before they get better, and that it will be heaven on earth only after Christ returns.

• *POSTMILLENNIAL*

This view states that the Second Coming of Christ will occur after the thousand-year-reign of Christ on earth. According to this view, the world will just keep getting better and better, thus ushering in the return of Christ.

The Return of Christ

• *AMILLENNIAL*

This theory states that there is no actual thousand-year-reign of Christ. The millennium occurs whenever a believer accepts Christ as his or her Lord and Savior, and that moment is when Christ returns.

So as you can see there are many ways of looking at this promised event. Whatever one chooses to believe about the Second Coming, there is good news: He is risen! He is coming again! Be ready!

The other day my wife asked me, "Randal, when are you going to get to the good news about the Book of Revelation?" I had been preaching this series, and she was complaining that I had lingered too long on the subjects of Mystery Babylon, the Antichrist, the Tribulation, and the battle for the church. I said, "Honey, this is it—we're talking about the Second Coming of Christ this week, and you can't think of any better news than that!"

I anticipate the Second Coming with great joy and expectancy. It can't happen too soon for me. I'm sure the disciples felt that way too. There they were, looking up as Christ ascended into heaven and saying, "Wow! This is some sight!"

Then the angels came and burst their bubble: "Why are you looking up? This Jesus who just disappeared into a bank of clouds will come again in the same manner; so get out there, get busy, go to Jerusalem, and do what He told you to do. Proclaim the Good News! He is risen, and He's coming again!" (see Acts 1:11).

Christ Jesus, the Son of God, born of a virgin, lived a sinless life, died on Calvary for the sins of mankind, and was resurrected Easter morning after three days in the grave. He ascended into heaven and is coming back in glory with His saints to judge the earth. Doesn't make a whole lot of sense, does it? But it makes no sense without the end of the story: He's coming again, and we win!

It's the simplest of all messages and the hardest to comprehend: He is coming again. And then everything will change. We'll have new bodies. There will be a new way of looking at things. All our priorities will be different. We'll be living in a new heaven and a new earth. We'll experience the joy of heaven. Everything will be different.

WE SHALL BE CHANGED . . .

Life on earth today is vastly different than the lives we'll lead, once Christ returns. It's as if we we're caterpillars, trapped inside dark cocoons. Life's not great, but it's not too bad. We have green stuff to munch on and it's safe there inside our tiny cocoons. Occasionally we become bored and peek outside. Out there, beautiful butterflies are flitting around in the sunlight. The light plays upon the colors of their wings, and the wings seem to glisten with iridescence. The sight of those butter-flies is so magnificent, it takes our breath away, and we exclaim, "Are those really butterflies? What would it be like to be a butterfly?"

One day a hole appears at the top of our

cocoon. We rise to peer outside, and there a butterfly meets us and proclaims, "You wouldn't believe the world outside the rim of that cocoon! It's beyond anything you could imagine! Out here, you'll fly—yes, fly!"

And what's our reply? "No way! Can't get out of this tight cocoon!"

But soon something strange begins to happen. We begin to shed our caterpillar skins and, in effect, die. The hole at the top becomes larger, and as the final wrapping of cocoon falls away, wings emerge and begin to flex delicately on the wind. Shades of brilliant blue and yellow create a glorious patchwork of color against the pale blue sky as many pairs of full-size wings unfurl. *We* are the butterflies! The caterpillars have ceased to exist. We have beautiful brilliant wings, and we are flying!

The Word of God says this about that moment to come: "In a flash, in the twinkling of an eye . . . we shall be changed" (1 Cor. 15:52).

It will be something like being transformed from caterpillars into butterflies on the day Christ returns, taking us with Him to live a new kind of life on a new earth. We can't even fathom how different it will be then or how wonderful. That's where faith comes in: We must simply accept that this is so.

Then I saw a new heaven and a new earth, for the first heaven and the first earth had passed away, and there was no longer any sea. I saw the Holy City, the new Jerusalem, coming down out of heaven from God, prepared as a bride

*beautifully dressed for her husband. And
I heard a loud voice from the throne
saying, "Now the dwelling of God is with
men, and he will live with them. They will
be his people, and God himself will be
with them and be their God. He will wipe
away every tear from their eyes. There
will be no more death or mourning or
crying or pain, for the old order of things
has passed away." He who was seated on
the throne said, "I am making everything
new!" Then he said, "Write this down, for
these words are trustworthy and true."*

—Revelation 21:1–5

One of the final End-Time battles that will be
waged against you is the enemy's last-ditch
attempt to keep you earth-bound. Satan would
like nothing better than for you to become so
rooted in the world's system that you won't long
for that new heaven. Can you see what I mean? If
you become earthbound, you will lose the Big
Picture. You will be unable to comprehend the
wonderful events waiting for you in connection
with Christ's return.

God doesn't condemn you for not being excited
about going to heaven. He realizes the pull this
earth has on human beings. There is a better way,
however, of looking at the Second Coming than
fearing it or feeling sorry to leave the earth behind.

Remember, earth is going to become increasingly more evil. The Tribulation will unleash a
horrible series of satanic attacks against mankind,
and the Antichrist will rule. So this is going to be a

horrible place to be. Who would want to stay? Yet there are two views. The earthly view is just what can be seen down here. It involves the mark of the beast, the Antichrist, and all the evil that will be unleashed on earth. The second view—the divine view—is filled with revelation. It's the view beyond the glass, and that's the view I'd like to close with. The divine view paints the Big Picture for us. It reaches beyond the bad news—that the earth is going to be a very bad place to be—to the Good News, and the return of Christ to reign for a thousand years of peace on earth.

That's the best news I can think of—in fact, the best news of all time. He comes just in time, after two-thirds of the world's population is overcome by disease, famine, war, and pestilence. Many will beg to die, yet will not be able to do so. The waterways will turn to blood, and the sun will burn so hot that the atmosphere will be unbearable. The ultraviolet rays will be so highly concentrated that cancer will break out everywhere, just by being exposed to sunshine. People will cry out for the rocks to fall on them and put them out of their collective misery. And then it will get ten times worse. People will die of starvation by the multi-millions.

The Antichrist will come and promise peace but deliver more oppression than any dictator in history. All this because people refused to allow Jesus to rule their lives. All this because man has insisted on destroying himself. Mankind would rather accept a demonic ruler than the goodness of Christ's lordship.

But believers have made a different decision;

they chose to accept Christ and to follow Him. When the evil hits, we won't even be around to see it happen. I believe we'll have been taken out by the Rapture. (Remember, I'm a pretribulationist.) And at the precise moment when the earth has been disciplined enough for her rebellion, Jesus will return, and we'll be right there with Him in the clouds. What a glorious day!

Now, you would think that when things really begin to get bad on earth, the people who are suffering would quickly repent and turn to Christ for forgiveness and salvation. Wouldn't you think that would be true? Yet the Bible clearly paints a different picture. People's hearts will become harder. They will become more stubbornly set in their ways. As many determine to continue to go their own way, a few will accept Christ as Savior, whatever the cost, even amid tremendous darkness and the persecution that will follow.

It's time to look at the End Times from the divine perspective because only then will we see the hold earth has on people. Only then will we see correctly what God is doing on earth. These events will happen—the Bible guarantees this. But how we go through them will be determined to a very large degree by what we decide right now. What will it be—God's way, His perspective—or earth's way, and more hardness and difficulties? And even as the hardships associated with being persecuted for our faith heat up, God is saying, "Be encouraged! I have you right in the palm of My hand. It's tough out there, but no one can take you out of My hand. Don't worry; I'll protect you."

The Return of Christ

THE ONE WHO PAID THE PRICE

Jesus is coming for His Bride. He has already paid the price for her, redeeming her from sin and her life from destruction. That price was paid in full two thousand years ago on a cross at Calvary, and ever since He has been preparing His Bride to rule at His side throughout eternity. We are that Bride, His church.

He lived for us, pointed out the way for us, prayed for us, died for us, rose again for us, promised He would come for us, and has ever made intercession for us at the right hand of His Father. He loves us beyond any human capacity to understand such a love. But we see Him through a glass, darkly, unable to understand how anyone could possibly pay such a price—or why anyone would want to. We are, after all, fallen flesh, full of darkness and desperately wicked short of His redemption.

Yet here we are, the Bride—desperately seeking her Husband. We have been made righteous and pure, and we're anxiously waiting for Him to come for us in holiness, with "faithful and true" written on His thigh. He is the Son of God; He will not send a counterfeit. He has promised to come, and He shall surely fulfill that promise. Nor will He ever leave us. We will see Him and worship Him in true adoration, face-to-face, just as promised in His Word. We will live in a new heavenly city where there will be no sin. Can you imagine?

Right now on earth, we struggle to live holy

lives in a polluted atmosphere where sin abounds. When Christ returns, it will be like the Garden of Eden once again. We will be able to achieve the will of God without the lure of sin, and we will rule and reign with Him. The lion and lamb will lay down together, and peace will crown creation.

Words can't possibly describe what God has in store for His people when that day finally arrives. Today we stand outside the glass, our faces pressed up to its coldness, trying to get just a peek. Then we will be beyond the glass, no longer spectators, able to see Him face-to-face in all His glory.

A FEW FINAL WORDS ABOUT HIS RETURN

The first word I have for you regarding the return of Christ is simply this: *Trust Him.* We are not living merely to survive the End Times. We are living to press through and trust Him, what's ahead is in fact far better than what we have right now. And one day we shall behold these things.

The second word is this: *Serve Him.* What concerns me the most these days is that we make the church serve us rather than serve the church and in so doing, serve Jesus Christ. We forget that He is a God who rewards our faithful service. Some of us would rather have our rewards right here and now. Yet the best rewards will be given to us in heaven. God has far more rewards waiting for us than we can possibly comprehend, if we will just forget about when and where and how they'll come—and serve Him.

The Return of Christ

My final word to you is, *Expect Him.* Be ready. At any time. He's coming soon. Live a life devoted to Jesus Christ. Look beyond the temporal pleasures of this world and take it by faith that Christ is coming soon. In the meantime, know that there are rewards for serving Him and for looking forward with expectation to His coming. Whether or not those rewards come to us now or later in heaven, is actually irrelevant. If we're just in this for what we can get, then we'll miss the joy that comes with serving Christ wholeheartedly. He has something better in store for His children than anything the world could possibly offer.

Not too long ago I gave my wife a brand-new wedding ring. The first was a diamond so small you had to use a magnifying glass to see it! It was a family heirloom that had come from my mother's side of the family. My mother wore it; then my wife wore it. I couldn't afford anything better than that as a preacher on a salary of fifty dollars a week, so that was the ring I gave her on our wedding day. Then we began to have children. Next came saving for their college funds. Finally, with the children taken care of, I went out and bought her a ring. I made a very big deal out of presenting it to her. This one, after all, didn't require a magnifying glass! It's the ring I wish I had been able to give her the night I proposed to her. I planned my presentation to take place in our favorite restaurant, with the band playing our song. At just the right moment, a waiter came to our table and presented her with a bouquet of roses. I said, "Honey, I love you," and gave her the ring. With tears in her eyes, she said, "Thank

you, sweetheart, but you didn't have to do it!"
However, she didn't give back the ring!

Why should she? The beautiful new ring com-
memorated not simply our many years of marriage
but the best years of our lives together. It signified
commitment and faithfulness, in addition to our
love. As we sat there in the restaurant preparing to
leave, she said to me, "Honey, some day we'll be
in heaven together with our children and our
friends. There will be no sickness, no sadness, no
sorrow, no misunderstandings." As much as I love
my wife and as happy as we were that evening,
we could both clearly see that Jesus had something even better in store for us than the joy we
experienced that night.

As my granddaddy used to say, "You don't
know what awaits you. In a cloud, He will come,
and we shall behold Him—our Savior."

> *Then I heard what sounded like a great
> multitude, like the roar of rushing waters
> and like loud peals of thunder, shouting:
> 'Hallelujah! For our Lord God Almighty
> reigns. Let us rejoice and be glad and
> give him glory! For the wedding of the
> Lamb has come, and his bride has made
> herself ready. Fine linen, bright and
> clean, was given her to wear' . . . Then
> the angel said to me, "Write: 'Blessed are
> those who are invited to the wedding
> supper of the Lamb!'" And he added,
> "These are the true words of God."*
>
> *At this I fell at his feet to worship him.
> But he said to me, "Do not do it! I am a*

fellow servant with you and with your brothers who hold to the testimony of Jesus. Worship God! For the testimony of Jesus is the spirit of prophecy."

I saw heaven standing open and there before me was a white horse, whose rider is called Faithful and True. With justice he judges and makes war. His eyes are like blazing fire, and on his head are many crowns. He has a name written on him that no one but he himself knows. He is dressed in a robe dipped in blood, and his name is the Word of God. The armies of heaven were following him, riding on white horses and dressed in fine linen, white and clean. Out of his mouth comes a sharp sword with which to strike down the nations. "He will rule them with an iron scepter." He treads the winepress of the fury of the wrath of God Almighty. On his robe and on his thigh he has this name written: KING OF KINGS AND LORD OF LORDS.

—Revelation 19:6–16

Holy is His name!

Epilogue:

ARE YOU READY FOR HIS GLORIOUS RETURN?

Only those who know Christ as their Lord and Savior will experience the joy of meeting Him in the air and seeing Him face-to-face. Only those who have recognized their need of such a Savior will spend eternity with Him when He comes again. Do you have this most important of all of life's issues settled within you? Are you ready to meet Him if He were to come again today?

If your answer is no, or if what you feel is fear and not joy and expectancy each time you consider His coming, will you pray this prayer with me? Once you settle the issue of your salvation, you too can experience the joy of His coming:

> *Jesus, I need You. I can't do this on my own. I admit that I fear Your coming, and I admit that I can't say for certain whether or not I will spend eternity with You. I want to spend eternity in heaven, so I ask You to forgive me for my sins. I repent, and ask You to fill me with the Holy Spirit in preparation for what You are about to do on earth. Prepare me to meet You, Lord. Fill me with Your peace, and the confidence that comes with knowing that salvation is Your free gift of grace and that it cannot be worked for or earned. I accept that gift, by faith, as I make You not only my Savior but my Lord. In Jesus' name I pray. Amen.*

Congratulations! You just made a decision that will forever affect you. First John 1:9 states, "If we confess our sins, He is faithful and just to forgive us our sins and to cleanse us from all unrighteousness" (NKJV). Chapter 5, verses 14 and 15, further promise: "Now this is the confidence that we have in Him, that if we ask anything according to His will, He hears us. And if we know that He hears us, whatever we ask, we know that we have the petitions that we have asked of Him."

See you in heaven!

About the Author

RANDAL L. ROSS is senior pastor of Trinity Church in Lubbock, Texas, and is host of *Answers for Today's World*, a daily radio and television ministry heard throughout West Texas and New Mexico.

Since Randal Ross became senior pastor, Trinity Church has grown to more than ten thousand members. An interdenominational fellowship, Trinity Church has special programs and ministries for youth, college students, and senior citizens including Trinity Christian Counseling Center, Trinity Christian School, Heartline Center (a crisis pregnancy counseling center), and Heartline Apartment Complex (homes for unwed mothers).

He is also a keynote motivational and leadership speaker on the international conference circuit for several universities and Fortune 500 companies. As a speaker, his goals are to help men and women reach their full potential for Jesus Christ and to raise godly leadership throughout the world.

Pastor Ross and his wife, Andrea, have been married for twenty-two years and have two children: Matthew Lee and Jessica Ann.

Other Books by Randal Ross

SEVEN HABITS OF WINNING RELATIONSHIPS

NOT WITHOUT MY CHILDREN

TAPPING THE POWER OF YOUR EMOTIONS

TO CONTACT RANDAL ROSS, WRITE:

TRINITY CHURCH
7002 CANTON AVENUE
LUBBOCK, TEXAS 79413